A
DIVINE
WORD
FROM A REVELATION

A

DIVINE

WORD

FROM A REVELATION

RUBÉN GABRIEL

God is Longing for the World to Listen to His Message

TATE PUBLISHING & Enterprises

Published by Tate Publishing & Enterprises, LLC
127 E. Trade Center Terrace | Mustang, Oklahoma 73064 USA
1.888.361.9473 | www.tatepublishing.com

Tate Publishing is committed to excellence in the publishing industry. The company reflects the philosophy established by the founders, based on Psalm 68:11,
"The Lord gave the word and great was the company of those who published it."

Book design copyright © 2010 by Tate Publishing, LLC. All rights reserved.
Cover design by Amber Gulilat
Interior design by Blake Brasor

Published in the United States of America
ISBN: 978-1-61663-490-2
1. Religion, Christian Life, Inspirational
2. Religion, Christian Life, Spiritual Growth
10.08.02

Acknowledgements

Praise and honor be to God the Father for giving me another day, to Jesus who paved the way for our salvation, and the Holy Spirit who never let me go astray. They are the best friends I could ever ask for, without them, none of this would be even possible.

My wife, Karla Iliana, who believed and understood me, my son Jan Karlo who has helped me come closer to God with a childlike manner, my son Mateo who through him I understood that God is with me even in the storm. Both my parents who never doubted my ability and because of them, I came to know the Lord. My brother, Daniel, my sister, Anna, and her husband, Victor, who have been very supportive and cheering me on.

I give you my eternal gratitude for having faith in me.

To my family who help me appreciate life all the more, to my friends who have never let me down, to my brothers and sisters in faith who stood by me.

Thank you for all your support.

I would like to thank the team at Tate Publishing that put this book together.

Table of Contents

Foreword

When the revelations of God are made simple and easy to understand, it's like eating a delicious dessert that doesn't overwhelm you, but rather you enjoy it, savoring it in your mouth for just a little longer. This book is that dessert so scrumptious that you will enjoy it even more the more times you read it. Psalm 119:103 states "how sweet are your words to my taste, sweeter than honey to my mouth." You will be filled with encouraging thoughts and in return your life will begin to change for the better. In this book are God's words that our lives sorely need. They bring peace in midst of the storm, it is his voice calling out to us, "I am here, let me help you, let me be a part of you." As you read his words, it will change the way you see the Spirit of God, the third person in the Trinity, the loving Spirit that wants to befriend you, and be your companion so that he can take you to new heights in your relationship with our Lord.

—Ruben and Patricia Valle
Senior Pastors, Valle de Saron

Preface

August 12, 2007. Sitting on the floor in the middle of my room on mid- afternoon, I found myself crying out to God. I was searching for answers to all my questions, my body ached, and my mind seemed clouded; I was in desperate need to hear from God. My soul needed him more than ever; there seemed to be a battle inside of me, and I felt that I was on the brink of defeat. There was a sense of urgency, a sense of longing that I hadn't felt before. I was twenty-seven and my life had been a selfish journey; my prayers had been one-sided and my life needed change. There was more to life, there had to be. I was happy and productive, but it was all superficial. Inside me was a war, a desperate war that needed God to intervene. I had been baptized by water and fire; my Christian roots were established but not very well developed. I wanted to know God more intimately than anyone else, I wanted for him to speak to me like the prophets of old. My soul needed this, I longed for him, I missed him, and I couldn't stand it anymore. That moment, I realized that I wasn't as close to God as I wanted to be. I needed answers but not from other people—I wanted answers from the Creator. Minutes seemed like days, and I prayed earnestly. I tried to imitate prayers from those who said they spoke to God but still no answer.

From sitting I went to kneeling and I knelt there in silence. For once, I had stopped talking and started listening. I began to feel his love around me, hugging me, embracing me. Suddenly, a voice, speaking from within me; I could hear him. I could feel him, and I realized that it was he, my God, my love. I scrambled around the room until I found some paper and a pen. I began to write all that he told me, I began to write all that he said. I realized that day that all this time I had tried to listen to God through my carnal ears but my soul hadn't been submissive to his Spirit. The Holy Spirit had been active and alive in me, but it was not until I learned how to silence my ego that I was able to listen. He had been talking all this time, but it was I that didn't give him the attention he deserved. I felt peace fulfill my inner being, and the more I listened, the easier it got to understand what was being said. My mind became clear and my heart content and my soul seemed like if it had been reunited with a long lost friend. It was the beginning of a beautiful friendship and ever since then, I have always yearned for more.

That day marked my reunion with God. The funny thing is, Jesus had already done that for me a long time ago. In fact, he did it for everyone except we tend to undermine what he did for us, and we don't value the price he paid. He has left the Holy Spirit to guide us and teach us everything we want and need to know. It is through the Spirit that we can listen from God the Father, Jesus the Son and of course, the Holy Spirit. Everyday I had an appointment with God, and all I did was sit there and listen. Sometimes it was in the morning or evening prayer, other times when I was driving and others when I least expected it. He spoke to me in his house, in the garden, at the movies, at work—everywhere and anywhere, he spoke. So I began to carry around a notebook and a pen everywhere I went.

Before we begin let us clear some misinterpretations about God. God exists as a Trinity; intertwined within each other through each other is God the Father, God the Son, and God the Spirit. The Holy Spirit is the one that dwells in us and speaks directly to our soul. He was given to us after Jesus redeemed us through his death on the cross. We are all children of God and we all possess God's Spirit within us but that doesn't guarantee our salvation. Only through Jesus can we receive the seal of the Spirit of God; giving us access to God's kingdom. The Spirit is the only one that can hear and speak to God. So I invite you before we begin our journey to let the Spirit of God pour out his wisdom and open your eyes to the truth. There are prayers if you so desire at the end of this book to help you start a relationship with God the Father, Jesus and the Holy Spirit.

Introduction

The time has come for the world to change; the time is near when everything will be made clear. Darkness seems to cover the land but hope is not lost. The Light still shines brighter than before. Some have given up and others have lost the way. We cannot stay in darkness any longer; we have been set free. God is still calling out his children to come and enjoy the feast. The Holy Spirit is trying to lead us back home; it doesn't matter where we came from or what we did, what matters is where we end up. Our goal in life is clearly set before our eyes, but we somehow still miss it. There is a war within us trying to lead us away from the truth. We must not give up hope; we have already won, except most don't know it. We are fighting a battle that has already been decided, we are stressing ourselves when we have been given rest. The journey is long but the prize is greater. We are being called to march, and so we must answer or we can just sit here and wait for life to swallow us up. We are ordinary so that God can be extraordinary.

The world is a busy place, full of responsibilities, full of deadlines, full of distractions. We work so that we can play, but then we play too much that we forget to work. Time becomes our keeper, and we are governed by our inability to manage it wisely. We usually go about in life waiting for something to happen, but yet we hardly put our own efforts into creating, and we spend our time waiting. We feel useless, trying to find a meaning to life, something worth living for—but can there be such a thing? Is there such a treasure that cannot be measured? Is there something hidden but yet revealed only to those who dare to look beyond human understanding? The soul perceives it, but the worldly mind does not want to believe it, and our mind convinces our flesh that this is it. We only live once and when we die—we will perish. But no, the soul is consistent in convincing the mind that there is more, more to life, more to live, more than death. We must quiet our intellect and let pride stand aside. Listen to your soul, which in return will only whisper the secrets of life. Your soul is the temple from which the Spirit of God can break through. God speaks through his Spirit everyday but your soul has to open the door to the will of listening.

When we pray, we must also take time to listen. Prayer is not a monologue, rather a dialogue. God always has something to say but he never raises his voice. If we would just sit still and live, we would be able to see that God has never left. You can feel him with every breeze. You can smell him in a flower, but better yet, we can hear him within ourselves. We must be willing to learn, we must be humble in his presence to recognize him when he speaks. Let us remember that he is our King, and we should treat him as royalty. His Son has removed any barrier that was in our way to reach him. We don't need to schedule an appointment for his attention; we don't need an extensive resume to have him hear our pleas; all we need to do is believe. Don't trample the blood that was shed for us by his Son. Jesus made us worthy when we were unworthy. It is a prideful boast to be called sons of God. The Holy Spirit shows us the way into the secret depths of God, but we must be willing to follow. I cannot tell you that the path is effortless, but I can tell you that the path is rewarding. God is looking for people to listen to his voice, and better still, people who will follow his divine purpose in their lives. How can someone made of flesh and bone understand the Almighty? His ways? His love? But maybe, just maybe, if you are willing to take the step of faith, you can listen to God speaking softly everyday in your life. He wants you to know him, he wants you to understand him, and he wants to be in every aspect of your life.

Why? Simply put, because he loves us so much. We are the ones that complicate love. We put doubts and what-ifs, why and who, we spin ourselves out of the sweater of love and comfort that God made for us with his own hands.

These revelations are for everyone, whether you believe in God or not, whether you go to church or not, these words are meant for you. His words are meant for increasing our faith towards the unseen, enhance our love for him, display our respect towards one another, but in the process you will also get to know our Creator. The Spirit of God is within everyone, but he is a gentleman and will not force himself into your life. You have to invite him, and he will help you value what you read. Let God love you; let his love and grace flow in your life. Let his teachings and commandments be a part of you. So, I invite you to let all your doubts go and just trust in the Lord our God. He is speaking to us, and I have learned that when he speaks, it is best to listen. God loves to speak in simple terms so that everyone could understand but yet that simplicity is still so complex, so we must yield to the Holy Spirit who will in turn translate everything to our soul so that our flesh can also benefit. God cannot go against his Word, so it was important to note that each scripture is used as a guide before each revelation to open our eyes as to what he is telling us and to remind us of what God had previously told us before.

Prologue

These words are not mine. I am just a conduit for God; he speaks, and I listen, and so I write with his permission. We joke and laugh until I understand, and then his grace makes me see what a disgrace I was before I met the one who made me. His Son I hold up high; he is my King and my love. I pledge my life to him who gave up his for mine; I was a sinner, and yet he still loved me as if I was a saint. I have a friend who I hold very dear, he has shown me the way so that I won't be led astray. The Holy Spirit, who shines from within, holds my ways, and when it seemed that I had gone a different path, he still held me by my hand. These revelations are his voice that echo through the land, written for the world but not of this world. We sometimes stumble, but through his love and mercy he shows us the way. Our desire must transpire through our heart and mind, through our words and actions; we must want him as much as he wants us. I am just a conduit for God, but in the process we became friends. And as a friend, I must do what he asks of me, to show you the way into his heart. These letters are his love put on paper and all that I can ask is that you won't hurt the one who made you. I am just a messenger like you, and my message is simple. Believe and hope. You have nothing to lose and everything to gain. In here, you will hear his voice, you will find his calling but you will also find the true purpose of your self.

—Rubén Gabriel

Part I: August

Change

This is what the beloved Lord says to the world:

And no man putteth new wine into old bottles: else the new wine doth burst the bottles, and the wine is spilled, and the bottles will be marred: but new wine must be put into new bottles.

Mark 2:22 (KJV)

8/12/07

"If you change then they change. Change is necessary in your life, if not, I can't finish my work in you. You ask for change, then I'm going to change you. We must get rid of all the things in your life that hinder our relationship. I was going to do it anyway, but it is easier for you when you are willing and aware of what is happening. Usually you are surprised at the process. What did you think? That I could use people that want to be great with their impurities, no, change is necessary. Do you want to be my servant? Then you have to change your old ways. Don't take it wrong—change is vital. It's just that sometimes you think everything bad happens to you and it's not like that. I can turn anything that comes against you to your favor. Do not be discouraged, sanctification is a lifetime process. You'll understand how everything works later but for now just trust in me, just trust. Is it to difficult what I ask? You must trust and not doubt that good things are going to happen in your life. As surely as the moon sets, I will always love you. Change can be hurtful but very beneficial; unfortunately you can't see the finished product until after it is finished. If you want to change the world around you. I must start with you."

The Mute

The Spirit of the Lord God is upon me; because the Lord hath anointed me to preach good tidings unto the meek; he hath sent me to bind up the brokenhearted, to proclaim liberty to the captives, and the opening of the prison to them that are bound;

Isaiah 61:1(KJV)

"What are you afraid of? Of what people are going to think? I am the one who judges; you have to get rid of that shyness and fear of speaking my Word. Little-by-little we're scraping away that fear. Later it will be easier to talk about me, but it only gets better with practice. Why are you afraid? What holds you back? Do you want to save souls from their obvious lack? Then you need to talk. I don't need a mute; I need a person who talks, that talks about my kingdom, about Jesus, about me (the Holy Spirit). Do you want to hear me? Then listen. Do you want to see? Then open your eyes. I love everyone, and I need everyone, but I need everyone to talk. You will see that the more you talk, the more you will realize that it is not you who is talking but me."

Insecure

I am worn out waiting for your rescue, but I have put my hope in your word. My eyes are straining to see your promises come true. When will you comfort me?

Psalm 119:81–82 (NLT)

8/13/07

"Everyone is blessed in me. Whatever happens, I take care of you, and I let things happen. Your body is weak but your spirit is strong. I need workers that work not just people who say they work. I need people who pray not just people who say they pray. I need to cure your hearts of wickedness, and I need for you to do my will. What is wrong with the church? How many times do I have to repeat myself, listen, follow, and see my power in your lives. You complain but you are blind, you doubt but you don't pray. There are so many things I want to reveal to you, but you don't let me. There are so many wonders that I want you to see but you don't wait for me. Patience is gold, love is precious. Insecurity can be profitable, because all you need to do is bring your insecurities to me. When someone is insecure about something, they don't know where to go and they have a choice of many different paths that they can take. It is easier this way because my path is always present and you can follow it easily. When someone goes down the wrong path, then they have to turn back in that same path and fight against the same doubts and worries that pertain to that choice. Then you end up in the beginning that is me. You follow the right path after going the wrong way, unfortunately that is the way you are. You don't learn good from good but rather

24

good from bad. Why do you have to be in poverty to see riches? Because that is the way you learn to appreciate. Why do you have to live in sickness to be healthy? Because that is the way you learn to trust in me. Wouldn't it be easier to live in riches, in health? Yes, but sometimes I use your weaknesses so that you can learn to depend on me. Nothing bad is going to happen, believe in me, trust in me, confirm it with me, I am with you, and if I am with you, nothing can be against you. You can see the waves of sin approach, but they won't touch you."

Die Only to Fight

I am crucified with Christ: nevertheless I live; yet not I, but Christ liveth in me: and the life which I now live in the flesh I live by the faith of the Son of God, who loved me, and gave himself for me.

Galatians 2:20 (KJV)

8/14/07

"What is the difference between today and tomorrow? You could live for me today or die for me tomorrow. What is the difference between the birds that fly and those that don't? That they fly because I permit them to fly. I need you. Take advantage of today; the day is always worthy of your time. Today is good for living and good for dying. When I live in you; your self has to persistently die. You have to give me your life, your dreams, and your will, and I will convert them into our life, our dreams, and our will. That is how I can guide you, when you turn in your life to me everyday. There are things that you have to do that you won't understand. There are things that you have to see that you won't believe. But that is the way things are, because no one will ever understand the things of God while living in the flesh. The Spirit sees the things of the spirit; the flesh sees the things of the flesh. Your sinful flesh must die, and you must learn to live in Spirit. Paul understood this concept, but he still struggled with the flesh, like you. Let my will be done in your lives, day by day, hour by hour, and minute by minute. There is no rest, there is no 'break,' like you say, there is no one-hour lunch. Everyday, every moment, the Spirit does not rest, the soul does not sleep, just the flesh which is weak. Do you think that the devil rests? Of course not, he is always attacking. Fight and win everyday. The war is on whether you want to believe in it or not. The war is on whether you fight or not. Is it not better to fight than to beg for your life? I need warriors, I need generals, I need captains, I need soldiers, and I will wait for you. Lift up my sword and yell; lift up my Word and don't rest. There is no rest. To rest is to accept defeat, and my children are never defeated as long as they fight with me. I give you the weapons of love and of wisdom to fight against temptation. I never said that winning is easy; there are sacrifices that have to be made. Obedience is costly, praying is costly, waiting is costly, but all worthwhile. Everything is worthwhile and when you see the beauty of heaven then you will understand why there is a war. The adversary doesn't want you to come home. The lost souls are not with me, because no one would fight for them. You just wait for me to come but what about them. It's okay to wait, but what are you waiting for, if I am already in you, and I say go and fight for the lost sheep. Fight for your land, you are not from here but live here. You belong to me, fight for the New Jerusalem, fight for her, lift up your banners of love, of self sacrifice, of faithfulness, of obedience, of wisdom, of revelation, of fear of me, and lift them up high so that the enemy can see. They will yell with fear when the earth shakes and they see my powerful and immense army coming after them. I need you to be a part of my army, the fight is unbelievable but essential, a lot of souls will be saved and a lot of souls will be lost. But those who died for me will also be raised in me, I am the steadfast rock, and I cannot be moved. Stand firm in me, that the battle must be fought in your heart."

To Pray

But we will give ourselves continually to prayer, and to the
ministry of the word.

Acts 6:4 (KJV)

8/15/07

"You have to come to me day and night, it is good to pray in the
mornings so that you can start your day with me, but it is also necessary to pray at night so that you can end the day in me. I am the
Alpha and the Omega, the beginning and the end; you don't know
what is going to happen tomorrow, so it is better for you to end your
day in the arms of your Lord."

Three Levels

For he will repay everyone according to what that person has done:

Romans 2:6 (ISV)

"There are three levels in heaven. All three are allowed only through the acceptance of the grace through Jesus. The first level is for those who believed in what I did for them but never really made an effort to know me. They were content with the conformity of life. The second is of my followers; they followed me and were faithful to my Word, they prayed, listened, went to church, and always tried to do my will. They were grateful for the gift of redemption and they showed it through their actions. The third is that of my workers. They left everything to follow me; they sacrificed their lives for me, their time. Their love for me was so much that they sometimes forgot about themselves. They knew what I wanted before I asked them. They brought the lost back home. I have crowns for everyone, some are more beautiful than others, some more amazing than others, but you are all my children, and I love you. I wish everyone could see the crowns that I have reserved just for them. But just the way you would like to brag about what I am going to give you, that is the way I need you to go after the blind, the mute, and the deaf. Don't be selfish with your gifts but share in what I give you. Only through grace is everyone made worthy to enter the kingdom. Flaws don't matter; your weaknesses don't matter. It doesn't matter the way they have treated you; everyone deserves to be in my kingdom. I don't want the flesh; I want their soul. Be merciful to those who think they need nothing from me. They think like that because they have never tasted my blood. When you taste my blood it will always be in you, you have to drink and fill yourselves up everyday. I love you. Jesus of Nazareth."

Give

Do not love the world or anything in the world. If anyone loves the world, the love of the Father is not in him.

1 John 2:15 (NIV)

8/16/07

"What is it that you suffer so much for me? Beatings, mistreatments, what is the complaint? Obedience is costly; is that what you suffer? What is the complaint amongst yourselves that you suffer so much for me? Do you think you suffer more than I suffered for you? I don't think so. Then why are you grief-stricken? Because I ask you for more? Because I ask you to do things you don't understand? What is the distress then? Do you need to see the prize before the race so that you can be more comfortable? Believe me the prizes are there. The more you give the more I give you. I give you so that you can help in expanding my Word to the ends of the earth. Do you want to be known for your love? You must give what the master gives you so that you can represent his name to those who don't know him. Share everything you have, what do I mean? Simply to give, give time, give love, give wisdom, give money; the more you give the more I give you. Just because I don't give you the things you ask for that very moment, well that doesn't mean I don't want to give it you. It's just that everything is in my time, but I always give. Everything is mine; you have to understand that. The faster you understand this principle the faster you will learn to provide for others. This has to be a test you say? 'Is this the will of God?' You ask yourselves, of course this is the will of God, helping those in need is always my will. Listen because I am speaking, open your eyes because I am showing you, the people of this world measure themselves by how much they have, but my children are not measured by their material possessions, they are measured by the amount and disposition to give. This world has an illogical concept of measuring true wealth. You cannot take anything with you when you die, and absolutely nothing from this world is transferable. Let go of your love of money. This world perverts itself when it makes you think that this is the only way to have significance, but I never showered myself with gold when I was here. I never lived in earthly castles but rather with a humble carpenter that had to work to feed us. I was still the son of a king but of the King of kings, so don't worry I have control over everything; nothing is out of my control."

Unbelief

8/17/07

"There are two types of unbelieving people. The first are the ones who believe in my promises, and keep on believing, and finally they give up hope, because they grow impatient and frustrated and say that 'This was not from God anyway.' Their impatience is their downfall. The second type are the ones that receive a promise from me, but they discard it immediately. They don't believe. The words might have brought them peace at the moment and they give thanks for the promise, but deep inside they don't care to believe. They may even believe it for a day or two but it quickly dwindles away. Which is better? To believe and give up or simply never to have believed at all? When you don't believe at all, doubt fills your soul, and like I've said before, doubt can work for your benefit. With time the unbeliever will reach a point in which the troubles of this world will cripple their arrogance. They will look for me, maybe, because they have nothing else to lose and in reality they have no other option but to wait on me. I am always at your house looking for a way in so that you won't have to travel far to find me. Of those who believe and then fail to maintain their faith, it is a little harder to persuade them to believe in me again. They feel that they have wasted their faith, their time, and their sweat. They believed in something, but they wanted their response to be answered quickly and most of the time their response was just around the corner. You cannot dictate how you want your prayer to be answered; you can only trust that I am always willing to give you something better than you expected. I never make you pass through fire so that you can get burned. I pass you through fire so that all the impurities can be washed away. I am with you guiding you in every test, every time. You become pure only through me, but you never seem to see that—you give up so easily. Don't ever give up. I am always here waiting on you. You may think you have control over the situation, and you can try to pass through it alone and even then I will help you or you can just give me your worries and wait patiently on me. This is the only way you can get rid of all the anxieties that stand in the way of my peace, to leave everything to my doing. Don't depend only on yourselves; you'll only lose your time. Leave your worries to me. Don't be impatient with the unbelievers, they will come to me and then they will look for you, but you have to keep on talking about me. All you have to do is plant the seed and watch it grow."

The Duty of a Christian

Be devoted to one another in brotherly love. Honor one another
above yourselves.

Romans 12:10 (NIV)

8/18/07

"What is the responsibility of a Christian? What is the duty of a
Christian? It's simple, all you have to do is spread my Word, don't
stay seated, but rather get up and talk about my kingdom. Talk about
my love, my mercy. I show mercy to those who ask for mercy. A
hardened heart only inflicts pain to everyone around them including
one-self. Many people don't know that they have a hardened heart
and they don't listen to my guidance and my voice they ignore. If
they only came to me and asked for forgiveness, if they only opened
their eyes, they would be able to see my love for them. If they would
only listen to my voice through my servants, if only, if only. Talk
about me, the little you know is more than what people that don't
know me know. How difficult can this be? Don't you talk about
movies, about last night's fight, you talk and talk about so many
things but yet you forget to mention me. This is a duty of a Christian, amongst other things; to speak about me is one of the most
important and less selfish acts. You want to walk in love, then you
have to respect one another, forgive one another, and help each other
in the time of need. There are so many things that are required of
my children. Be sure that when you do help, don't do it for your own

selfish reasons. Don't say, 'If I do this, then Jesus will surely reward me,' but rather just do it for me, because I am in you. If I guide you, then how would I handle that situation? I will never make you do things you can't do, but when you think the things you can't do are doable through me, then I am always willing to help. In this world, you are used to seeing bad things happen and then you shake it off with a 'I'm glad that didn't happen to me, thank you God, for not permitting anything like this in my life.' I am not saying that you shouldn't be grateful, but what I am saying is that you should go out and help that person in need. I don't ask anything big, nothing you can't handle. Simple things like giving someone a ride to work, cutting someone's grass, taking out the trash, inviting them to eat, little things that don't seem to matter, but they will matter to me and the person you helped. Don't look for praise from the world, rather look for the praise from your Father in heaven and have him thank you personally for your help and doing his will. With time, I will ask for more help from you, bigger projects, more people, but everything in due time. For now, concentrate on the little I give you to do, so that I could give you more. If someone asks you to borrow something of yours, lend it, but don't expect them to pay you back. I will pay you back for the good you did. If someone asks for help, then help, and I will help you. Most of the time you have pity on people that need help and your concern is of no good if you don't do anything about it. You deceive yourselves and think because you had pity on them and prayed to me about them you did all you could but when you had your chance, you let it go to waste. You could of helped them out with a little money, which by the way is all mine, but you leave that place with a false sense of love saying to yourselves 'If only I could of helped.' I help those who help those in need. What is the duty of a Christian? To live in love."

My King

Come near to God and he will come near to you. Wash your hands, you sinners, and purify your hearts, you double-minded.

James 4:8 (NIV)

8/20/07

"Why is it so difficult to find me in your lives? What is it about your daily routine that you're unable to hear me? You don't have time for me; you don't make time for the King. I need your full attention. How many times do I have to repeat myself? In what form or way do I need to express my desires so that you can see it is I who is talking to you? I love you, but I need you without a blemish and pure. But how can you be pure if you don't obey me? How can you be perfect in me if you don't listen? I gave you my Son to make you faultless by placing your faults on him. Through his death you can come so that I may enjoy your company. Make time for me, make room for my Word, make space for my love, but also make room for one another by teaching each other how to listen to me. I can speak easily to you whenever I want, and I can make sure that you listen, but this is not how I want to do it. I want you to want to listen to me; I want you to want to follow me. I want people that leave their uncertainties and follow me. I want workers who listen and that know how to listen to the silent whisper that blows like the wind in their heart. Can you see me in your lives? Can you see the health in you that I give you? Can you see me in you and you in me? The kingdom awaits and you don't have to be looking, you don't have to say 'Where are you,' in order to follow me. I am in you, in your heart, but you have to stay still and listen to my voice. Just be patient and you can listen to my love. Where am I? I am in you. Where am I going? I will go where I take you but you need to surrender your will to me, if not, then we cannot walk together. I will try to take you with me but you will push me away, you will say, 'I know the way Lord, follow me,' but now you are mistaken. The created cannot know more than his creator, now it seems that you always knew the best route. When does the servant surpass his master? Never. You have to understand that I know the better way, whether you like it or not, you can't do it on your own. You think you can, but you can't. If I only took away a little of my grace from you, you would be in ruin, my grace sustains you, don't be proud. I have control, I guide you in everything but I need you to trust me. I need you to turn your lives over to me completely, not in part, not one day yes and one day no, but everyday. I want to bless you but you must be willing to accept the changes that I must make in you. Let me be your King in your life."

The New Church

So it is with you. Since you are eager to have spiritual gifts, try
to excel in gifts that build up the church.

1 Corinthians 14:12 (NIV)

8/21/07

"What am I doing in your life? I am purifying you through me, I
am molding you in my image, and I am scraping off all the sins that
are in you. I need a wise and strong church; I don't need foolish
talk amongst yourselves. I don't need a weak church; I don't want a
church that doesn't fear me. I need you to submit yourselves to me,
and you will see all the wonderful gifts I have in store for you. My
church will be known throughout the world and the whole world
will know that this is my church. From here workers will set out and
do my bidding, and I will give them power unlike any other that has
been seen before. Ideas will flow that will revolutionize. New laws
and agreements that will edify and change the route of the current
church will be implemented. I need you to understand the immense
proportion of influence that you will have on the world around you.
Many people will see you and want to be like you but you need to
set a good example as of now. There will be manifestations of the
Spirit, there will be healings, revelation like never before, miracles of
many sorts, and people will wait night and day just to get a glimpse
of my glory in my church. I need prophets, teachers, pastors; I need
everyone of everything because the movement is coming. You will

be like my disciples, in that you will be united, tied together with my love. You will share what you have with each other, you will break bread together, and you will pray and fast together. You will love and cry for those who are lost. I will be among you, sharing every step of the way. You will be judged and criticized by men. You will be humiliated, but forgive them for they do not know that I am the light of this world and of the next. People that don't know me will say that this is not from God but I tell you that it is. Don't be afraid to be different. Don't be afraid of the world. As long as you are guided by my Holy Spirit you will not depart from me. Pray for those who hate you, bless those who curse you, forgive the blind and the mute. While I am with you, who can stand against you? The enemy will try to make you doubt; he will try to deceive you because he is afraid of the power that rains down on you. My movement will be so massive that the church will tremble. Not because it might fall, but because of all the people that will rush to it so that they can see and listen to my voice as I heal the sick. All this will be so normal for you that you will soon forget how hard it was to get here."

Rich in God

"Therefore I tell you, do not worry about your life, what you will eat or drink; or about your body, what you will wear. Is not life more important than food, and the body more important than clothes?"

Matthew 6:25 (NIV)

8/22/07

"What is money? Why is money so important in your lives? Do you ever question me in regards of why there are poor and rich people? Why does it seem that I give everything to someone and to others I give nothing? Are you not satisfied with my presence in your life? The one who has me has more than the ones who don't know me but thinks he has everything. Would you rather be rich without me or rich within me? If you belong to me, you cannot belong to the world and since you don't belong to the world then you can't be measured by the world's standards. You are measured by something greater; you are measured by your love, by your helpfulness, by your obedience. You say that without money you can't find happiness. Why is that? How is that even possible to lose your happiness because of money? Open your mind and realize that you are not a slave to money but rather a caretaker of money. Do you see the children playing in the rain? Who bought the rain? Do you see the children playing outside? Who bought the sun? You, with all your money, can you make the birds fly? You, with all your money, can you give life? Your money is worth nothing where I am not present. I give you everything you need, and my promise is kept; food will never be scarce in your house, and you will always be clothed. You have to trust me. I am free to give and I give freely to those who seek me. Do you really need brand name shoes? Do you really need a luxury car? What is a brand name? What is luxury? These are the things of this world that distract you from me. You measure yourselves and set your own standards but you exclude me. I am luxury and greatness. I give and I take. Ask me in my Son's name and I will give it to you. I am always a cheerful giver. If you were to seek eternal riches then I can trust you with earthly riches. After all you are my children. If I decide not to give you what you ask for, don't complain; I always have something better for you. Everything comes in the order in which you believe. Faith moves my hand."

The Test

Consider it pure joy, my brothers, whenever you face trials of many kinds, because you know that the testing of your faith develops perseverance.

James 1:2–3 (NIV)

"There are tests that have to be made in your lives. You come to me with great passion and you ask for a radical change in you, 'Change me o Lord, change everything that is impure in me, I want to be clean.' So then, I begin to change what is needed in your life and what happens, you begin to criticize my work, you start to complain instead of being grateful. Do you think that when you ask for faith the heavens open and fire pours down on you? Do you suppose that the wind comes blowing through your window and suddenly while you're praying you are lifted up into heaven and just like that you receive the greatest faith on earth. Well, I'm sorry to disappoint you, but it doesn't usually work that way. I can if I want, but you need to learn how to trust me. I put circumstances in your life and instead of viewing them as obstacles, in reality they are opportunities. I stand back and watch you trying to figure out why this has happened, and I'm hoping that you will realize that nothing depraved ever comes from me. So you begin to trust me and abide in me, and you begin to grow while you are in crisis. While you're in fear, while you're in doubt you come to me, because you know that I am your Father, and everything begins to come together for your benefit. You will always know where your home is at the end of the day."

Holy Spirit

And I will ask the Father, and he will give you another Counselor to be with you forever-the Spirit of truth. The world cannot accept him, because it neither sees him nor knows him. But you know him, for he lives with you and will be in you.

John 14:16–17 (NIV)

"Pray silently and take some time to meditate on my Word when you read it. Let my Holy Spirit guide you with each prayer and whenever you sit down to read let my Spirit lead you. He knows every single letter and the meaning of every single word. Who do you think inspired the prophets? Ask for his guidance, all you need to do is ask. Wake up with him everyday and go to sleep with him every night. He is your personal guide, and he resides in every single one of you. Don't mistreat him and don't ignore him. You have to understand his power; you have to fill yourself with him before you talk, even before you pray. He will give you courage when you fear, he will give you wings when you fall, and he will help you trust when you're in doubt. I let him come down for one reason, so that he could guide and transform you into my image. He is the creative force in our power. He is the creative force in you. There are so many people that misjudge him and tend to forget about him, because they think he is not an important part of the trinity. We are all one, he is me and I am he. Open your eyes and you will see."

Anger

A fool gives full vent to his anger, but a wise man keeps himself under control.

Proverbs 29:11 (NIV)

"Why are you so quick to anger? What is it really that you gain from getting upset? I understand it is an emotion and God gave everyone these emotions. Jesus got upset, Paul would get angry, Moses, everyone eventually gets upset? But what is anger? It is an emotion that comes from within you, and it is sinful when it becomes uncontrollable. There is a difference between getting upset and staying upset. There is a difference between forgiving and holding a grudge. There is a difference between anger and rage. In your grudge people stop forgiving and maintain themselves away from the others. What do you gain by this? What do you lose? Is your way of being and pride so important that you lose days and sometimes years before you even talk to him or her? All you do is waste your time, and you let pride run through your veins like poison that it consumes you. The longer you take in forgiving, the harder it will be to forgive or to ask for forgiveness. What do you lose when you don't forgive? Love, the kind of love that holds you together now seems to separate you and doesn't let your soul rest. Is it worse when you're the one at fault? Now, you're not only including yourself in this whirlwind of anger, but you have included more people. The same way that you are hurting yourself you are also hurting those around you. You can't act like children and throw a fit when people don't listen to what you say. You have to learn to love each other. I cannot base my church solely on emotions, that if something upsets you, I am the one you get mad at. That if you feel discouraged then you don't pray. If you're having a bad day you forget about the one who can brighten it up. That you're upset so you don't preach or you don't feel like blessing yourselves. Let me give you rest and relieve your burdens."

Jesus Lives

He was delivered over to death for our sins and was raised to life for our justification.

Romans 4:25 (NIV)

8/23/07

"I was sacrificed for your sake; I carried the sins of the world with me. I died and was resurrected. You do know what it is to resurrect? It means to bring back to life. If I am alive then why do you still have me crucified? Haven't you heard that I am no longer dead? I am your king; I don't need your pity but I do need you to fear me. How is it possible for me to live in you, and you in me if you still have me up on a cross? I am Jesus all powerful. I have made you righteous. I have made you in my image. Everything you were has died with me on the cross. Let us live a new life in harmony and love. I am alive and I am coming back for my sheep."

The Word of God

"As for God, his way is perfect; the word of the LORD is flawless.
He is a shield for all who take refuge in him."
2 Samuel 22:31 (NIV)

8/24/07

"There is an aroma of love that flows through my Word that is unseen by the naked eye. You can't feel it, and you can't taste it, but if flows like a river through you and it washes you with the fountain of life. My Word is not a book; it is a way of life. My Word is me, and I am the Word. You can't read it like a book, you have to read it like if getting to know me. I have revealed my plans and my love for you in my Word. You have to memorize the scripture, so that you can edify each other with them and my Word will continue to flow through you. You have to make time to read everyday; a son of mine has to get to know his Father. Do you want to know me? Then all you have to do is read. I am in every page, I am in every word, and if you can't see me all you have to do is ask the Holy Spirit to show you. He will make you see what is unseen, and he will light my precious jewels that are hidden in plain sight. He opens your eyes, your mouth, your ears, so that you can understand and teach my Word to the world. Meditate on it, just like you needed to be fed in order to grow when you were a child; that is the way you need to be fed through the Word in order to grow in me. Without my Word you are defenseless in this world, but with it, you are undefeatable. Eat from my Word, drink from my Word; it is life for the obedient and death to those who don't believe."

The Voice of God

My sheep listen to my voice; I know them, and they follow me.

John 10:27 (NIV)

"How can you listen to me? In silence, in your thoughts, in your actions, through your own words you can listen to me talking. I speak through anything and anyone, but don't shut me up. I come like a soft summer breeze, but you don't take time to listen. I am in your thoughts, but you don't want to quiet your mind. You begin to doubt, and say 'It is only my imagination.' What is your imagination? Do you not think that I exist in your imagination? How do you want me to come to you? Do you need lighting, earthquakes? No, I come to you softly in a voice that you can recognize in order for you to listen. If I talk to you in the way you want me to, then you would probably be frightened every time you would hear my voice. I talk to you through your own voice, but you still doubt. I talk to you through others, but you still doubt. I talk to you through signs, but you still doubt. I talk in so many different ways, but you don't care to listen. You have to train your soul to want to listen to me. Flesh listens only to flesh, but I am Spirit, so your soul needs to talk to me in spirit. You don't need to sit for hours waiting for me to talk, but you do need to sit there loving and wanting to hear from me. Take a second from your busy life, and tell me that you want to hear me. I am willing to talk to those who are willing to listen. What is the difference between those who hear me and those who don't? Is that some want to listen with their carnal ears, but the others know how to listen to me through their soul and from my Spirit I will speak. Without my Holy Spirit it is impossible to listen to me; without my grace, it is impossible to listen to me; without my love, it is impossible to listen to me, but I give you all this freely. You don't have to beg for my love or my grace, but you do have to ask the Holy Spirit to be a part of you. Can you see the way the wind blows across the leaves of the trees and how they move majestically? That is the sound of my voice moving through your life."

Time for God

"And you, my son Solomon, acknowledge the God of your father, and serve him with wholehearted devotion and with a willing mind, for the LORD searches every heart and understands every motive behind the thoughts. If you seek him, he will be found by you; but if you forsake him, he will reject you forever.

1 Chronicles 28:9 (NIV)

8/24/07

"What events are in your lives that are in the way of spending time with me? How is it that some can dedicate more time praying and others can't? Don't you have the same amount of hours per day? Don't you have the same amount of minutes as everyone else? You make up excuses and blame it on everything and everyone else except yourself. You are the only one standing in your way towards me. You are the only one responsible for not making time to be with me. I wait for you, and I knock at your door, but you have to get up and open that door. You don't have to wait for me to arrive because I am already here and I'm waiting. You seek answers; you seek help; you seek advice, but you don't seek the source to all your questions. I am the answer. I am your help. I am your advice, your God all-powerful. Your flesh is weak and the burdens of this life are heavy. Come to me and rest your sorrows, seek my comfort and don't lose hope. I came to make my house in you but of what use is a house that is unkempt and unloved. I need you; I need your will to be aligned with mine.

I made you in my image so that you can love me but you must seek so that you may find. I Am in every hour, every minute, everywhere you go and everywhere you'll be, I Am in you. Take an hour, take whatever time you want to spend with me but just spend it with me, and we will walk together in this life and the next. I Am the answer to your questions, I Am the answer to your doubts, and I will carry the load for you. I died on the cross for you so that your sins could be forgiven; so that you could enjoy a lasting relationship with the Holy Spirit. I have a covenant with you, so don't take my death in vain and take advantage of the presence of my Spirit. I give it freely to all that ask, just come to me. Forget about tomorrow; forget about yesterday. In this time we are one and all is forgotten. I forgive everything but you must ask. The only thing flowing through us is our love for one another. Close your eyes and kneel, and you will see that I Am."

I Came for the Sick

"It is not the healthy who need a doctor, but the sick. But go and learn what this means: 'I desire mercy, not sacrifice.' For I have not come to call the righteous, but sinners."

Matthew 9:12–13 (NIV)

8/26/07

"There is a void in you that cannot be filled with the material things of this world. Money will never satisfy you, power will only spoil you, nothing can completely fill your joy the way I can. For everything that has ever happened in your life—for all those times you said you were okay, for that false peace that you hold—you are absolutely alone if you don't have me. Those who have everything have nothing; those who seem to have nothing have everything. There is pain in those hearts, there is desperateness in those feelings of uncertainty, and there is frustration in your flesh, so why don't you give me your burden? You don't have to carry the burden; you don't have to walk alone. I will walk with you. There are so many people that don't know me, there are so many people that spend their lives trying to figure it out, and there are so many that lose precious time just trying to proof to themselves if I exist. I am the light and the way. You don't have to walk around blindly in the darkness. It's easy to open your eyes, it is simple just to turn on the light, all you have to do is follow me and never again will you be by yourself. For those who commit adultery, for those that commit crimes, for those who hurt, for those who lie, for those who cheat, for those assassins, for those unbelievers, for those prideful, and for those who say they don't need me, I am here waiting for you. Don't let your sins stand in your way of true happiness. I forgive all sins except one; grieving the Holy Spirit. I died for you. I came for the sick, for the drug addicts, for those who are poor in spirit, for the drunkards, for the thieves. I came, and I died for every one of you—no one is free from my grace. I fill your spirit with fire that soothes your heart. I fill you with water that runs through your veins and gives you life. Don't be afraid and don't fear; I will never reject you. Here you are welcome; I wait for you in my Father's house. My Father has made his house in you, but you have to break free from your ego. You don't have to live in pain, I am the life, I am health, I am the way, and no one can come to the kingdom if not through me."

Give Thanks

You are my God, and I will give you thanks; you are my God, and I will exalt you.

Psalm 118:28 (NIV)

"I want you to open the windows of your house and watch how the trees swing back and forth, how the birds fly, and after you have witnessed the simple things in life, you can give me thanks. Thank me for giving you one more day of life. Thank me for giving you the time to spend with your family and friends. Thank me for everything that I have done in your life. I made everything; enjoy life with everything that I have given you. Sometimes you go through life so fast that you forget how beautiful the sunrise is; you forget how beautiful the moon shines down on you and how the clouds sometimes hide behind the rain. Take time to breathe. Take time to value all those things around you that glow with their different colors. If you love the world, then you will learn to love me, because I am this world. I am in the wind, in the earth, in the leaves, and in the rain. There is nothing here where I am not present. You can feel me when the wind whispers in your ear—when the rain caresses your hair, I am there. Take time to appreciate what I have made for you."

The Love of the Christ

Because of the LORD's great love we are not consumed, for his compassions never fail.

Lamentations 3:22 (NIV)

8/28/07

"Love is fragile. It has to be nurtured and watered. It has to be maintained full in order to survive. Love comes and then it goes; love falls and then it gets up; love doesn't have words; love doesn't listen; love doesn't see; love is a feeling that you embrace with smiles, that you feel with joy. Love holds you up with its gaze. It is the most beautiful thing, without limits, without goals and it can't be held in a box. It is free and given with care; it also hurts and it also cries. Love is a flower that has to be kept in the palm of your hand. You protect it from the rain, and from the wind. It fills your soul with an aroma that is sweet to the heart. My love is perfect, my love is so immense that it can't be measured; love itself cannot contain the love that I give freely. I give it to you so that you can give it to others. My love doesn't hurt, my love doesn't distrust, my love is faithful, my love is powerful, and my love is everything you ever wanted to come true. My love holds your hand when you think you're alone, my love guides you when you seem lost, my love gives you water when you thirst, my love takes care of you when you fear; my love protects you from temptation; my love is perfect, and my love is in you, because I am in you. My love is only shared by you—my love is for you.

My love is for everyone that wants it and even for those who don't seem to care for it, I still give it. My love is without limits. My love doesn't have rules and spins the world. My love moves my Father. My love's pureness cannot be understood. My love is holy and filled with power. My love for you is not in vain. I wait, I search, I invite, and I guide you into my love. My love cannot be contained in these words. My love cannot be measured in a book. My love is for everyone and everything."

The Warrior

Endure hardship with us like a good soldier of Christ Jesus.
No one serving as a soldier gets involved in civilian affairs—he
wants to please his commanding officer.

2 Timothy 2:3–4 (NIV)

8/29/07

"Flesh gets weary, but there is also weariness of the soul—when one
grows tired of waiting for me, when one gets tired of praying and
sees no physical results. When one grows frustrated of everything
that seems wrong in their life, there is weariness. But in that weariness, victory is just around the corner, if you could of just have waited
a little longer, if only you would of prayed just a little more to hear
my answer, if you just would of taken that last step when it seemed
that you were doomed to fall. My Spirit brings life into your weakness and fills you with a desperate cry for me that you will say, 'I will
not give up, Father I am not giving it all up when I am so close. Give
me strength to finish the race. It doesn't matter how many times I've
fallen; it doesn't matter if I'm hurt or if I can't see the finish line. I
know that I am not alone, I know that your Spirit guides me.' I will
turn to you and see that you have seen human failure and you have
felt disheartenment. You have passed through deserts, but still you
follow me, bleeding, yelling but still staying on course. You have followed me until the end. You have suffered for my name's sake, and
I will brag about you. I feel proud to be your Father. For those who

have fallen and have risen; for those whose heart is that of a lion's and for those who would rather die than to stop following me. These are my warriors. Whatever comes into your life you are not alone. Nothing that happens in your life is out of my control. If I am in control of everything, then why do you worry? A warrior never gives up. A warrior only sees the finish line and that is a victory in itself. Dress yourself with my Word and protect yourself with the blood of Jesus. Get wisdom, join forces with love, and we will continue to march. My army does not know surrender, my army does not fatigue, my army dies for their King. Do you think you can die for me? Do you think you can give me your life in complete disposition to do my will? Can you put me before you? Can you stop doing your will and give me your total trust? What is the difference between a follower and a warrior? A follower thinks he can do everything and a warrior already did it."

Cost of Disobedience

See to it, brothers, that none of you has a sinful, unbelieving heart that turns away from the living God. But encourage one another daily, as long as it is called Today, so that none of you may be hardened by sin's deceitfulness.

Hebrews 3:12–13 (NIV)

8/30/07

"What is the consequence of disobedience and abandonment? Hell. It fills me with grief when my children don't believe in the existence of hell, that there isn't punishment. They blind themselves with lies and begin to believe that by simply ignoring the enemy he will vanish and the only alternative will be to come to heaven. It is sad to see those who think they could do whatever they want and not suffer for it. Hell exists; the enemy roams the earth and is waiting for you like a hungry lion. He hides himself with every word, disguised in laughter; he waits patiently to devour your dreams. Anger turns to rage, a conversation turns to gossip, a misunderstanding turns into a fight, do you think this is all mine? Do you think I like it when you get revenge, that you curse and then bless, that you envy, no, this is not of my likeness. What do I permit then? I permit a certain situation in your life to make you more aware of my presence. I permit certain things to happen so that you can grow and be filled with me but evil doesn't come from me. You are the author of your own consequences by your disobedience. I utilize what you caused to teach you. After all, through trial and error you learn quickly. The enemy is also always looking for a way to inflict pain in your life but remember who is on your side. In conflict, you can shine your strengths as well as your weaknesses. Everything that you see badly, I convert it to good. Every decision you make is totally free but you have to be guided by the Holy Spirit so that you won't fall into any traps of the enemy. The deceit of sin is making you think you are not in sin. The deceit of sin is making you believe that Jesus wasn't enough to save you. The Holy Spirit will sanctify you through the repentance of sin. Pity on those who don't believe in heaven or hell, there are so many without direction. They think that beyond science there is nothing else. I Am the answer to all your questions, and I need you to show the world that I Am the Creator, that I Am the all-powerful. I made man in my image, and I blew life into him. It hurts me to see my children lost, it hurts me to see them stray from the truth. I need workers that want to work; I need servants that are willing to listen to me. I need you to go after my lost sheep and leave those ninety-nine behind and find those that are lost in the wilderness. Not every war is fought with a sword but all of them are fought with love."

You Have To

Do not conform any longer to the pattern of this world, but be transformed by the renewing of your mind. Then you will be able to test and approve what God's will is—his good, pleasing and perfect will.

Romans 12:2 (NIV)

8/31/07

"You have to learn to leave your problems in my hands. You have to learn that I have control of what happens in your life but you decide where you want to go. You have to learn that in order for a situation to change, I have to allow it. You have to learn that your decisions can't be based on your feelings. You have to learn that everything you do must have a higher purpose and not in vain. Learn that it is sometimes better to stay quiet than to speak. You have to learn to see the love that there is in every one of you, even the most hated is still capable of love, even the lost still want to smile. Listen to the melodies that I put in your heart; learn to smile instead of crying, because you know you are not alone. Sometimes you have to cry to understand the pain of your fellow brother. Learn to breathe in life that so quickly fades away. Appreciate a hug that is given so scarcely from your loved ones. Conquer the world in my name, give a kiss every time that you can and learn to say, 'I love you' without rest. Learn to ask for forgiveness and forget your pride so that you can be happy. Look for me and you will find everything. Once you find me, don't look away so that you won't lose yourself. Learn to ask and you shall never want. Learn to depend on me, and you will see that you don't need yourself to rely on. Learn to sweat to work and then make work sweat for you. Leave everything to have everything. Be innocent and humble so that you can learn. My way is hard on the flesh but easy on the spirit; it is not for the weak but rather to make the weak strong. You have to die to live and you have to forgive so that you too will be forgiven. Learn that you are not perfect in order to be perfect. Learn that you are a sinner so that you won't sin any longer. Pray to be in my presence, only through the Son can you reach the Father. Be friends with my Spirit so that you can learn to listen. Learn to give thanks so that you can receive your blessings. You have to give to receive and quiet your mind to listen."

Part II: September

The Root

Preach the Word; be prepared in season and out of season; correct, rebuke and encourage—with great patience and careful instruction.

2 Timothy 4:2 (NIV)

9/1/07

"What is behind that mask that you wear? What is behind that feigned smile that only hides suffering? In order to understand fear you have to dig towards your heart. I will show you the hearts of people so that you can see the pain that tortures them everyday, and you will pray more efficiently for them so that you can attack the problem from the root. People laugh but cry. People dance but suffer. People want but don't know how to ask. There are so many masks that people wear to hide their shame, to hide their pain, to hide their fear. If you really ask them hopefully they'll tell you themselves what is it that they feel so that those chains can be broken and they will be set free from their misery. People want to be happy but don't know how. Many people want to dance, but no one asks them. So many people want to help but don't know how to start. Ask me, and I will show you the hearts of my sheep. If you ask me, I will give it to you in my name. I love it when you ask me; when you look for me; when you want something that is of no benefit for you but rather for someone else. I give you everything freely, because you want to give to others as I do. Many people come to worship me. They pray;

66

they go to the altar; they begin to cry with joy; they fill themselves up with my Spirit so much that they can't contain themselves, and they even fall when the Holy Spirit touches them. But as soon as the service is over, they go back to their house and remain depressed. That is a root that must be torn off and life must be planted instead. Plant truth and wisdom and establish a stone that cannot be moved, which is my Word. Once the root is lifted and my Word set in stone in them, then they can go home and still enjoy my presence. Don't lose your way and your hope. There are many people that need your guidance, that need your love. All of you are my children, but some need more guidance than others. Be patient with them, remember that it is me that is in you, and I teach you everything."

I Am Not in Feelings

For I am convinced that neither death nor life, neither angels nor demons, neither the present nor the future, nor any powers, neither height nor depth, nor anything else in all creation, will be able to separate us from the love of God that is in Christ Jesus our LORD.

Romans 8:38–39 (NIV)

9/03/07

"I am in your dreams. I am in the wind. I am everywhere, whether you feel me or not. I am with you in school and at work; I am with you while you drive and while you sleep. You don't always have to feel me to know that I am here. Don't let your feelings confuse you; your feelings can't always tell you when I am with you. Do you think I am more or I am less present if you don't feel me? Do you have to feel love to know that you are in love, of course. Do you have to feel anger to know that you are angry? Yes. But you don't always have to feel me to know that I am here, it can't be like this even though you want to. My power surpasses the flesh and your soul and goes straight to the Spirit. Your mind wants to feel and your body needs that reassurance that it is me who is talking to you. Your flesh is weak, but your spirit is strong, and if a strong wind comes, your flesh will fall but your spirit will never flinch. If a fire comes your flesh will burn, but your soul remains. When you die your flesh will rot but your soul will rise. I can heal your sicknesses, I can make the blind see, and the mute will talk, but first I need your soul to make communion with my Spirit. Remember in Spirit is where your soul listens to my voice and then in turn your soul directs the flesh where it needs to go."

Wake Up

For it is light that makes everything visible. This is why it is said: "Wake up, O sleeper, rise from the dead, and Christ will shine on you."

Ephesians 5:14 (NIV)

9/04/07

"Is there any doubt in you? This doubt goes around and around in your mind, and then it claws around in your heart until it finally blinds your judgment. It runs through your veins and begins to overtake you. But there are good doubts, and then there are bad doubts. There are good doubts that make you strive for more answers, and I reveal them as you continue on your journey. There are also bad doubts that make you drift away from me, when you begin to doubt my power and think that you can go ahead without me. When you doubt your existence and then begin to doubt my existence, until finally, you have no idea as to what it is you are doing here on earth. Some don't want to listen to what I have to say. And for some, it is not convenient to do so, because they will be exposed to the truth and frankly, sometimes you feel better living in a web of lies. It's sad when I hear my children say that I don't seem to interest them. You know you are wrong but yet you still blind yourselves and rather live comfortably in deception than joyfully in truth. Don't get complacent, complacency is the beginning of deceit, even those that know me fall in complacency. I did not send you into this world to be complacent but rather conquerors. The enemy will tell you that there is no war, that you are not a warrior, he will tell you that it is a waste of time to pray for others. Don't fall into that trap; don't let the enemy tell you that it is a waste of time to follow me and stop doing my will. There are so many people that need help but no one to help them. There are so many people that don't want to depend on me because they are ignorant on the fact that they have everything by grace, but there is no one to wake them up. I need workers that activate that faith that lies dormant in my children and have my Spirit wake up their soul. Dress yourselves for war; leave your comfort and follow me. I am Jesus of Nazareth, your general."

What Is?

The LORD gives strength to his people; The LORD blesses his people with peace.

Psalm 29:11 (NIV)

"What is faith? Can you feel or taste faith? Is faith tangible? Is faith an emotion or ability? It is the certainty of knowing that things are even though it hasn't happened yet, or has it? What is peace? Does wealth bring peace? Can the world give you peace? God makes his peace flow down through his love and even though things around you seem to fall and crumble, you still maintain firm and trusting. True peace knows that God is in control, that God only has good tidings planned for everyone. What is wealth? Money, fame, cars. What is wealth? Wealth is to have me in your heart, to have love flow through you, having true friends, having health. What is my Word—a book, nice poems, and stories, something to pass the time? My Word is full of life. It is breathing and active; it is the truth and dependable; it is a sword that cuts through your soul. It is I."

Ignore the World

For everyone born of God overcomes the world. This is the victory that has overcome the world, even our faith. Who is it that overcomes the world? Only he who believes that Jesus is the Son of God.

1 John 5:4–5 (NIV)

"Don't listen to the blind, don't give attention to the deaf and don't fear the mute. Have mercy on them that they don't know what they say or do. They are really lost. They will try to hurt you but forgive them. They will try to misguide you, but understand that they themselves are lost. Don't play their game, because they cannot win, so it is an unfair advantage that you have earned in their eyes. Have compassion on them, have patience, love those who don't love you, forgive those who curse you, hug those who hit you. Eye for an eye it is no more, tooth for a tooth it is not your job, let me be the judge. I don't need you to judge; I don't need you to curse them rather pray for them that I have mercy because they don't know whom they are fighting. They are defenseless; woe on those that rely on things of this world, woe on those who say I don't live among you, woe on those who curse and don't ask for forgiveness. Have mercy on them, I know it is difficult to forgive those who offend you, but this is the way it must be done. How many times have you wished to let your anger out and curse them and make them see that they are wrong, and then come back to me and ask for forgiveness? But a true warrior does not let the words of those against the war stand in his way, he walks in Spirit. Don't let disbelief ruin your day. Love the blind, help the deaf, and laugh with the mute. They need you even though they think they don't. Don't judge, don't curse, and don't waste your time arguing. I can defend myself and all you need to do is pray for them and talk to them with love. Ignore the words that try to trap you."

The Window

"In the same way, let your light shine before men, that they may see your good deeds and praise your Father in heaven."

Matthew 5:16 (NIV)

9/4/07

"Your life is like a window that others could see into, and they will try to find the worst of you and the worst that was you. They will compare themselves to you, trying to justify their actions and their disobedience. It is easy to criticize when you're ignorant and it is easier to point the finger when you're blind. I need your lives pure and stainless, pure and without sin because you have to set an example for others. I need that window that they use to peek into your life to be a mirror instead, a mirror that will reflect what they can be like with me as their Father. This mirror will make them see their impurities as-well as their sin, and they will feel ashamed for trying to judge you. Love covers many sins, and this love has to be given to everyone, even to those who judge you. You cannot fall as long as you trust that I will catch you. Pray for all those that curse you."

The End

"Look, I will come as unexpectedly as a thief! Blessed are all who are watching for me, who keep their clothing ready so they will not have to walk around naked and ashamed."

Revelation 16:15 (NLT)

"The end comes quickly and swiftly, and I need my bride to be ready to receive me. It will be truly terrible the chaos that will be unleashed on this earth. Mothers will kill their children and children will kill their parents. Misery will be around every corner and the people will cry out to me and will beg for forgiveness, but it will be too late. I will ask them, 'Where were you when I looked for you and you never opened the door? Where were you when I called you but you never bothered to turn around?' You preferred the commodity of this world over me, and now death is gripping you, and your flesh will have to suffer now in order to come to me. I will then know that you are willing to follow me. It will be horrible when the seals break; where will you hide? Look for me now, because you don't know the day I come. Don't sleep because I come like a thief, I come in the blinking of an eye, be ready the day is coming."

A Warrior

"If they listen and obey God, they will be blessed with prosperity throughout their lives. All their years will be pleasant."

Job 36:11 (NLT)

"Don't let doubt run its course in you; you have no time to doubt. You know what it is that the King requires of you, so just wait for your instructions. How many times do I have to tell you to do something, when I have already told you? If you only listen when I whisper then you will know what it is I want. Don't ask why, it is not your job. A warrior walks in certainty that his King never lets him down."

I Knock on Your Door and I Wait

"No one can serve two masters. For you will hate one and love the other; you will be devoted to one and despise the other. You cannot serve both God and money."

Matthew 6:24 (NLT)

9/5/07

"Money only brings temporary happiness, if any. When money unexpectedly arrives you sing and dance, you laugh and cry, and all this is all right but just remember who is the one that gave it to you in the first place. Who took care of you when you where lacking and who gave when you were asking? Your Father. Many forget me and replace me with money and begin to believe that it was only by their efforts that they were able to attain such amounts. 'God helped, maybe a little,' you say. In reality if it wasn't for me, there wouldn't even be a you. Don't let greed fill your heart and the love of material possessions become your master. Little-by-little, you forget to thank me and then you forget that I even exist. This is when things that seemed alright begin to take a sharp turn, all the peace you felt is gone and all the friends you had are lost. The farther away you are from me, the closer you are to the enemy. You welcome him with open arms and begin to drown yourselves with your own sin. The enemy begins to tie you with his lies, and after a while there is no escaping and you don't know how to free yourself. You begin to fight, you scream for help but no one comes to your aid. This is when you remember me; after you suffer, you remember who loved you when you had nothing. I loved you before your riches and before your fame. When you didn't have enough for a soda, I gave you what you wanted so that you could buy that soda. Even though you forget me, I never forget you. I am always at your door knocking and waiting for you to open it. It is so easy to forget your Father and even easier to let money corrupt your love for me. Even though you have never been a good friend, I have always been your best friend. Even though you left my house, I wait for you and send my angels to watch over you. I am always knocking at your door, in the rain, in the snow, at night and in the morning, in the heat, I am always there, waiting."

How Easy

And when he was come into the house, the blind men came to him: and Jesus saith unto them, Believe ye that I am able to do this? They said unto him, Yea, LORD. Then touched he their eyes, saying, According to your faith be it unto you.

Matthew 9:28–29 (KJV)

9/6/07

How easy it is when you know that your Father is in control, how easy it is to bring your problems when you know that your Father has all the answers, and how easy it is to wait on me when you make things that are complicated very simple. Things that are easy can suddenly become difficult. You can make the possible seem impossible. Don't limit me; don't compare me; and don't doubt my power, for I am your God all mighty and powerful. I open the seas; I let manna rain down; and I create everything. For everything there is a beginning and the beginning of rest is faith. Faith without complications, faith without limits, faith in its simplest form. Begin to develop your faith and soon you will see the things that aren't will be. How do come to have faith? Love, begin by loving me, I don't ask for anything complicated—just to love me. How do you come to love me? Coming and talking with me every day, letting me be your Father when you need someone to pick you up, letting your Father hug your worries away. Talk with me, spend time with me, let our relationship grow and watch it develop into a life of love."

Flesh, Fire, and a River

"I baptize you with water for repentance. But after me will come one who is more powerful than I, whose sandals I am not fit to carry. He will baptize you with the Holy Spirit and with fire."

Matthew 3:11 (NIV)

"There is a fire that is in you, a fire that cannot be contained no matter how much water is poured into it. That fire is mine, it is my will, and it is my love that burns from the inside out. There is no room for anything else, my fire will not let anything come near it, nothing can hide from it, and poison cannot run through this fire. In this fire there is passion, there is fear, there is mercy. How can this fire be in you and my river of life also flow through you? This fire is in your soul and my river is in your Spirit. Then what about the flesh? In the flesh emotions flow, weaknesses, doubts, but all three need each other. How? My river runs on love, the fire burns your passion, and your flesh obeys the spirit of passion. But there is also a war between the three. The Spirit puts a desire in your fire, and your fire tells the flesh, but the flesh is afraid and doesn't do it. Then the currents of the river flow stronger and your fire ignites hotter but still your flesh does not obey. This can also work in reverse, your flesh wants to do something that is against the Spirit and your flesh forces the fire to ignite and work for you but the Spirit is against you. That is why it is important to make decisions together, me and you. Between us both, we can think better but you have to be in accordance with the

Holy Spirit. Don't let your flesh decide or even your soul. When you pray and you feel my presence that is just your flesh telling you I am there. But I move through spirit and most of the time you can't feel me even though I am standing next to you. I let your fire burn with intensity when I come near sometimes, simply just to comfort you. It is more important to feed yourself through the Spirit, that is where I work, there is the secret of man, in Spirit you will see my power, you will sense my presence, you need to stop trying to hear me and just listen. You need to be quiet so that you can talk. Don't let your mind be your enemy, remember I am not in feelings, even when you feel nothing I am there, even when you seem to be still, I am moving."

The Lost Sheep

Let him know, that he which converteth the sinner from the error of his way shall save a soul from death, and shall hide a multitude of sins.

James 5:20 (KJV)

9/07/07

"There is a lack of respect between you, a lack of obedience is lingering among you, you have to learn how to love each other, and you have to learn to love those people that don't seem to merit respect. There are different types of respect. There is a respect you have for your boss, respect for a friend, respect for your parents, respect for strangers, and there are so many other different types of respect. You have to learn how to respect each other out of love, out of wisdom, and you have to learn how to teach with respect and love. If you begin to rebuke everybody for their lack of understanding, then the only thing you will do is push them away from you but if you can gently show them what to do then they will learn even more. Learn to respect the decisions that they make, even if it hurts you, you cannot impose your will unto them. You can only plant the seed and watch it grow as I water it. I cannot change the way a person acts or thinks if he or she is not willing to do so, so don't make it your obligation to change their minds for them. I know it is hard to watch others fall after you have taught them what I have told you, but sometimes it is the only way they can learn. Don't ever give up on them, because I will ask you face-to-face what happened to the people that you led and never went to pick up when they fell. It would be so much easier if everyone that heard about me would instantly want to follow me, but it is not the case. People are stubborn when they let their ego lead them. It is so easy to find me, yet you make it hard to look for me. My way is easy but it takes work, asking for forgiveness is easy and forgiving is even easier for me. It is harder to find the way when you are stubborn than it is to walk in it and once you walk in it you have to learn to keep your focus. Now that you walk in my path you become a threat and whether you want to or not you will be tempted into falling once again. Stand in me, I am the rock that never moves, stand in me, and you will never be left alone and if you fall, I will stretch out my hand to pick you up. I don't live in defeat, I am a conqueror, and if I am a conqueror, then that is exactly what you are. There is a path that leads you to my lost sheep. It is not easy, it is not lighted, and it is not paved, but you will find what you are looking for outside the conventional way. It is your job to go and rescue the lost sheep. You must travel through water, through nights, through heat and cold. You must climb mountains and run through deserts and you will suffer to save it. But when you finally arrive—thirsty, tired, and weak—you will have to carry it on your back and travel back the same road you came through. I will give you strength when you are weak, I will give you water when you thirst, I will give you hope when all seems lost, and you will smile upon me and I to you. I know this isn't an easy task, but the rewards are great. It is a soul that was lost, and now you have led it to me. I walk with you; I guide you; and I know that sometimes it isn't as easy as you expect it to be and I thank you."

The War in the Mind

but I see another law at work in the members of my body, waging war against the law of my mind and making me a prisoner of the law of sin at work within my members. What a wretched man I am! Who will rescue me from this body of death? Thanks be to God—through Jesus Christ our LORD! So then, I myself in my mind am a slave to God's law, but in the sinful nature a slave to the law of sin.

Romans 7:23–25 (NIV)

9/8/07

"There is a war in you, a war about control and power. The enemy tries to distract you with things that don't belong to me. He will put thoughts in your mind when we talk, he will surprise you when you read my Word, the enemy uses your mind as a weapon against yourself and against me. You can't let your mind wander, you can't let your mind be empty; the mind is the entry point of your evil desires. You must learn to control what you think, control what you say, think before you speak because there is power in words. Think before you act so that you will be able to listen to my Spirit and nothing else. Think before you answer any question so that you won't fall into the trap of the enemy. The mind must be conquered by you and surrendered to me. Our minds have to be one in order to march and fight. You can come to church, but if your mind is somewhere else, then of what use was it of you going? Of nothing, your physical presence means nothing if your mind is not alert and waiting to receive my Spirit. Feed your mind with love. Take care of what you watch, of what you hear, and of what you say. Even though nothing seems to bother you in the present, your mind absorbs everything and then it reminds you of the things that can hinder you when the moment arises. Your mind is your greatest weapon but can also be your greatest weakness. Ask me, and I will deliver you from the spirits that cloud your mind, and I will fill you with my Holy Spirit of power."

Three Things You Need

He who gets wisdom loves his own soul; he who cherishes understanding prospers.

Proverbs 19:8 (NIV)

9/9/07

"There are three things that you have to know, three things that you can't be without. The first is love. Love is what makes the world thrive. Love is what makes you forgive and forget. Love conquers the unconquerable and crumbles the unshakable. The love of God is immeasurable and incontestable. Love destroys sin and forgives. You cannot be without love and live. The second is wisdom, the wisdom of my Word, wisdom as to how I work. Once you have wisdom you can understand the incomprehensible. I understand there might be some things that are hard to comprehend, but with wisdom, you can decipher anything. Wisdom needs commitment and it also needs time. The third is faith, believing without seeing. Without faith, what is wisdom but a bunch of knowledge set aside to waste. Without faith, love cannot reach its fullest potential. You cannot doubt my will upon you. Only by faith can you see miracles in your life. Without faith, wisdom would only come to reasoning and I cannot be succumbed to reasoning. You can read all you want and even give me the benefit of the doubt of what I do, but you have to truly believe in me if you want me to move in your life. Faith that stands still leads to nothing. Wisdom that is not applied is wasted and love that is not showed is led astray."

To Reach Heaven

For thou art my rock and my fortress; therefore for thy name's sake lead me, and guide me.

Psalm 31:3 (KJV)

"How can you reach heaven? My way is easy but it takes commitment. My way is narrow, but the doors are always open. My way has a reward of a happy eternal life. How can you reach heaven? You can't do what you want to do. You have to surrender your life to me, receive Jesus as your savior and walk in Spirit. First: Understand that if you walk alone you will fall. The burdens of this world are many and heavy. I have control of everything, and the sooner you realize that, the sooner you will realize that you walk in vain if not with me. I can help you with anything and everything; you do not have to live your life based on emotion or chance. There is no luck, give yourself completely to me, your old self has to die, and I have to live, let my will be done. Second: So that I can be in you, you have to accept Jesus as your savior. There is only one way to come to me and that is through my Son. Without him you are blind and mute, deaf and insipid. He is your life; he stretches his hand and waits for you to look upon him. Ask for forgiveness and receive him, and I will forget of everything that you have done in the past. Third: You must learn to walk in Spirit. Walk in love and love your enemies. The Holy Spirit will guide you in everything you do or say. Let your decisions be consulted with him and together you will create a whole new world around you. Don't let the flesh conquer you but rather let the Spirit conquer the flesh. This is just the beginning of a Christian."

To Ask

"Ask and it will be given to you; seek and you will find; knock and the door will be opened to you. For everyone who asks receives, he who seeks finds; and to him who knocks, the door will be opened."

Matthew 7:7–8 (NIV)

"If there was one thing that you could ask of me and I promised you that I would give it, what would it be? Would it be something for yourself or something for your brother? Would it be something for the world, or something for a few? If I let you choose anything you wanted, what would you choose? Something with value or something simple? Something for love or something prideful? You are not Aladdin that you just rub the lamp and out I come granting you anything you wish. This is not how I work, but I do give you things that you ask for, simply because I love you. Sometimes it is not yet time for you to receive it, and sometimes I have something better to give you. Maybe you're asking for the wrong thing or your motives aren't in tune with my will but I always keep my word and give you things even though you don't realize it. I love to give. I love for you to ask, from simple to great things, things with flavor and things that cannot be touched. I give everything according to my will and purpose. You will not give a knife to a child or poison to a baby, because you know that those things will cause them harm. Therefore even if they beg for it, you cannot give it to them. A father cannot give ill gifts to those he loves; then you have to understand that I cannot give you things that I know will only bring harm to you, whether you understand it or not. I always have something better to give you, but you have to be open-minded and focus on what it is you are asking for.

Sometimes you have to open your eyes to realize that what you are asking for; you might already have it. Stand in the middle and look around at all the things that surround you and you will see that I am always willing to give. Even then, you're still blinded by your uncertainties, and still doubt of what I can give you. Don't forget what it is you are asking for because you might receive it in a way that you can only see it through faith, so then if you can't see it, you will be tempted into believing that I didn't provide. What if I give you what you ask for except that you forget that you had asked for it, who is to blame? You can't be upset for the things you don't have, because in reality, I don't have to give you anything. Some days you forget what it was you were asking for, and then you get upset for the things that you don't have but then you forget why you were upset and what you asked for. Don't ask me with the wrong motives, because you won't get it. Don't ask me for things that don't help you, because you won't get it. You have to learn to give yourself completely to me and when you give, I will give. Give me your possessions, and I will give you mine. Don't misunderstand the world, don't let it own you but rather understand that you are only a steward for me here. I have control over everything. You ask of me things which are never going to be yours, but I'll let you borrow them. You ask me for money, and I allow you to have money; you ask of me a new vehicle, and I provide you with it, but don't let them own you. You cannot take anything with you when you die, you won't need them. Yes, I give to those who ask; well, I lend it to them. Don't get upset if I don't lend you what you ask for, I always have something better for you. Why don't you ask for things that will really help you, like wisdom, strength, love, mercy, patience, and many others things that the list would be endless. They are always freely given from a limitless supply. These things that are not tangible will really be yours, and no one can take them away from you. When you ask of me things that strengthen you, then the things of this world will come to you."

The Battle

"With him is only the arm of flesh, but with us is the LORD our God to help us and to fight our battles." And the people gained confidence from what Hezekiah the king of Judah said.

2 Chronicles 32:8 (NIV)

9/10/07

"How many times have you wanted to give up? How many times have you let doubt ruin your faith? Everyone passes through that, not only to the weak but the strong as well, but it is your choice to let it ruin you. A servant of mine passes through hard times; a soldier has to be trained before going to battle. Disappointment is always around the corner; doubt, and insecurity, all these things tend to creep up on everyone. No matter if you are strong or weak or if you are rich or poor, everyone must pass through the fire. You can't have victory without conquering first, you can't conquer without fighting, you can't fight without training, and you can't train without going through training camp. You must come to me first. The first battle is won when you decide that you can't do it alone. You must learn that without me there is no real victory. After this, you will have to fight off doubts and stress, but you will no longer be alone. We will fight everything together, and you cannot lose as long as I am with you. I send my angels to protect you, and I march in front of you while you dress for battle. Let the King of kings guide you as a general guides his troops to war. You cannot and will not lose. My soldiers don't know the meaning of defeat, but you have to stay with me—stay in the light and don't wander into the darkness. You must learn to trust your general; he always knows the best plan for attack. Will it be easy? No, because it takes dedication and perseverance. But, if you were to get hurt, I will heal and protect you. Only what I want to happen will happen, so don't worry about tomorrow, because I carry you in the palm of my hand. Let's go to battle, don't worry about who is coming against us, the enemy is only as strong as you let him be. He has deceived you into thinking that you are weak, that you need to absorb all the arrows that he shoots. It is not like that. We attack, we conquer, and take over cities. We don't wait, we march, and our praises and music can be heard all around the world, the land shakes with our splendor and we yell, 'Hail the King of kings.'"

Remember

My comfort in my suffering is this: Your promise preserves my life.

Psalm 119:50 (NIV)

9/11/07

"In this date, I want you to remember all the families that lost their children, their spouse, brothers, nephews, grandchildren, friends, coworkers. Pray for them; they need your support. Even though they don't know you, you can pray for them for me to send my angels. They are my children as well, no matter how far, prayer can surpass any boundaries. There was much death on this day but there was also life. Many of who never knew me started to search for me, be it for despair or pain, for whatever the reason, the important thing is that they found me. Many children sacrificed their lives for others; and there is no greater love than those who give themselves for their fellow man. Many that died that day are here with me, unfortunately not all of them."

Not Everyone Enters

"I tell you the truth, unless you change and become like little children, you will never enter the kingdom of heaven."

Matthew 18:3 (NIV)

"It doesn't matter how much you suffer when you die, it doesn't matter if your death was quick or slow, in the end, a sinner is a sinner, and a servant is a servant. I would love for everyone to be saved, I would love for everyone to spend eternity with me, but it is not like that. People don't listen, people don't understand that this life is only temporary, and I Am is the eternal life. You have to make people understand that they are not going to live forever. One day you will die, and I don't want anyone to die without me. This is their decision, neither you nor I can decide for them. People have to come in their own free will. You have to intercede for the blind, for the mute, for the deaf, for those who think that there is no hell. There is a hell, and trust me, you don't want to go there. Why pass eternity suffering and tortured when you can spend it in joy and in love? Why choose the wide road when the only reward is death? Look for yourself, and you will find me. Choose me over everything else. There is no pain in my house, there are no tears of misery, there is no discouragement, there is no death, there is only life, and there is a joy that cannot be explained. I am here, my Son is here, my Spirit is here, and we will walk with you everywhere you go. There are so many beautiful things that I want to show you. I love you, and I would love for you to be with me. Talk about me, talk about my kingdom, there are so many people that don't want to listen to what I have to say."

Faith

Now faith is being sure of what we hope for and certain of what we do not see.

Hebrews 11:1 (NIV)

"Faith needs to battle in order to grow. Faith needs to be tested by fire, not to be burned but rather to purify and remove all the impurities that cling to it so that it can glow splendidly. What is faith? Believing in things that are not seen as if they were, right. Well then how can you increase your faith, with a magic wand? Praying? Do you think that if you pray to have faith all night, by the next morning you will wake up full of faith. No, faith needs to be run through circumstances that you will need to have faith in order to continue. There will be times in which the only way out is through faith, your strength, your anger, and your passion will not be sufficient to save you from your troubles. Your faith will rescue you, because you know that I am in front and that you are not alone. In order to live free, you need to live in faith and faith comes from recognizing my voice and hearing my Word."

Dirty

He does not treat us as our sins deserve or repay us according to our iniquities. For as high as the heavens are above the earth, so great is his love for those who fear him; as far as the east is from the west, so far has he removed our transgressions from us.

Psalm 103:10–12 (NIV)

9/12/07

"Open your eyes and you will see that you are in no means perfect. You have your faults and your weaknesses, your sins and your doubts. You can have so many things against you that it is sometimes difficult to find out what it is you need to fix. In this world, you will always be dirty—dirty of a malicious thought or some cursed words. You will always be filthy without me. There are sins that you commit that you don't even realize it anymore that you are sinning. Some of you have made sin a habit. When you come to me with all the dirt of this world, imperfect in your actions and weak in the soul; I will lift you up, and I will bathe you with my precious blood. I feed you life and change your worn out clothes, every day you start anew. When you come to me in complete submission and repent of all your sins, I forget about yesterday and a whole new day begins. The enemy will remind you of what you did, and it is up to you if you let him defeat you with regret. You will come to me and ask for forgiveness for the same sin, and I will tell you, 'Of what sin are you asking forgiveness for? You have been washed and cleansed of all impurities. Jesus Christ has paid for your sins and has made you righteous.' I know you feel weak, and I know you are not perfect, but I can make you perfect when you come to me, but you must come to me if you want to be cleansed. All day, every day, you must come to my presence, and I will dress you for battle. The Holy Spirit will always sanctify you but you have to submit yourself to his authority. Don't fear coming to me dirty and sinful; you must always be ready to be washed. Your sin doesn't matter, your weakness has no strength before me, your doubts can be tamed, and there no sin is too great for me to forgive except the grieving of my Spirit. How can you grieve my Spirit? By not accepting what I did for you on the cross. I forgive everyone. Your Father who resides in heaven wants to forgive. I will feed you love, and I will listen to you patiently. With my wisdom, I will guide you, but come to me every day. Don't let the day pass by without being in my presence. It doesn't matter how many times you fall, it only matters that you get up each time. It doesn't matter how dirty you are, the important thing is that you come to be washed. It doesn't matter if you don't feel like praying, the important thing is to pray. It doesn't matter how many times you ask for forgiveness, the important thing is to ask. I am always waiting with arms open. A father never turns away his child when he misbehaves but rather comforts him. There are times when we must talk and understand that it is my duty to make you see the wrong when you think you are right. My grace abounds so that you may live free from condemnation."

Rest

"Who of you by worrying can add a single hour to his life?"
Matthew 6:27 (NIV)

9/13/07

"You have to learn how to rest in me in the middle of your prob-lems. You have to learn that you decide if you want to worry or not. You don't have to be stressed out, worried, lost, if you don't want to. You have control over all this, and if you want, you can live a worry free life. This doesn't mean that there isn't going to be a situation that may tempt you into worrying, but what does change is your perspective towards the problem. You will have a different approach on that situation, and you will see that it doesn't bother you as much as before. How do you change your attitude towards problems? You have to learn to come to me, learn how to leave everything in my hands and accept that it is better if we work together You must deny yourself and let my Spirit reign in your life. He will guide you and give you discernment on any dilemma that may arise in your life. You will open your eyes of your spirit when you begin to appreciate him. You will open your eyes of faith, you will see my power run through your life in your favor, you will stop complaining, you will stop being frustrated, and you will rest in the middle of the storm. You will learn that I have control, and I allow everything, because everything is always for your benefit when we make decisions together."

Don't Reason

"Blessed rather are those who hear the word of God and obey it."

Luke 11:28 (NIV)

9/14/07

"You don't need to reason to understand my words. You can't be pessimistic if you want to listen to what I have to say. A Christian doesn't have time to rationalize. I don't need someone that stops to rationalize when I ask him for something. If I need something done, your job is not to ask why. You can't say, 'I don't think it's a good idea God, I think it's better through over here.' I won't be able to utilize you if you don't want to listen. There is a difference between reasoning and letting the Holy Spirit guide you through your doubts. Sometimes before you make a decision, you wait for me to confirm what it was that I asked of you and that's okay but you can't stay put either. A true servant doesn't doubt his master but rather trusts that his master knows what he is doing. Learn how to trust me so that I don't have to repeat myself. If you wait too long you will miss what it was that I needed. You ask for confirmation, but you don't listen. Do you have to understand the finale of what I need you to do in order to do it? You can ask me why, that's what friends are for, but it doesn't mean that I have to tell you. I know the reason you ask, because I can see your motives behind your heart. I know when you ask sincerely or doubtful. Wouldn't it be easier if you just obeyed what I say? Learn to trust me one-hundred percent, learn that I have control over everything. There is good in everything, even though you don't understand the how or why, but I need you to listen and obey. I need soldiers not attorneys; I need warriors that follow their general. Remember that you can't win the battle by yourself. I am your King, and your King doesn't need to explain himself."

Take Advantage

Why, you do not even know what will happen tomorrow. What is your life? You are a mist that appears for a little while and then vanishes.

James 4:14 (NIV)

"There is little time to understand. There is little time to open your eyes. Time is short and life passes by quickly. Take advantage to come to the Father every day, because you will never have this day again. Take advantage to learn from your Teacher, because the time passes—take advantage to befriend the Holy Spirit, because the day ends. You have to learn to love your neighbor as yourself. Learn how to say, 'I love you,' and 'I forgive you.' Don't hold anything against anyone so that you can live free. If you forgive you will be forgiven. Hold on to joy and don't ever let it go. Be a good guest to your company so that you will be received openly. Don't let a hug go to waste so that love can flow through you, and you never know when you will need one yourself. The days are counted, but the days with me are eternal. The past never changes, but don't let it hold you down. Whatever happened yesterday is forgotten when you ask for forgiveness. Come to me, and I will forgive and forget. Come to me, and I will gladly accept your company."

The Change Is for the Brave

Now the Lord is the Spirit, and where the Spirit of the Lord is, there is freedom. And we, who with unveiled faces all reflect the Lord's glory, are being transformed into his likeness with ever-increasing glory, which comes from the Lord, who is the Spirit.

2 Corinthians 3:17–18 (NIV)

9/15/07

"What have you learned that I haven't permitted? I guide you in what it is you need to learn in order to grow. I know you have a choice of what to read and when to read it, but there are some books that will just waste your time and some that will make you understand the way I work. When you finish with one, I always have another book waiting. My Spirit lights it up, and you will see it if you want to. I know what it is you need at that moment better than you. Knowledge doesn't have a price and you should take advantage to learn something new everyday. If you ask for wisdom, I will help you, but you also have to help yourself by dedicating time to learn. If you ask for patience, then the world around you becomes your classroom, and I provide a situation in which you will need to develop patience. If you ask for change, then you have to prepare yourself because I will purify you and you will know that it is me. Be ready to receive when you ask because I am always willing to give. Be careful what you say, because the power of the word is incomprehensible. Be careful what you do, because you will reap what you sow. Everything has a benefit or a consequence. Don't ask for things that others have but rather ask for things that you need. Don't ask for things just to please the world but rather ask for things that will help you help the world. Change is necessary for your growth, and you should not fear it but rather embrace it because gold needs to be put through the fire so that it could be purified. I polish you so that you could glow with splendor. Take the first step and let me work in you. My warriors cannot be afraid of change; they have to dedicate themselves to learning from their mistakes. You can't put your new you in your old self."

Talk with Me

The LORD would speak to Moses face to face, as a man speaks with his friend. Then Moses would return to the camp, but his young aide Joshua son of Nun did not leave the tent.

Exodus 33:11 (NIV)

9/17/07

"I listen to all your prayers, no matter if it's night or day, no matter if you're by yourself or in public, no matter if you pray crying or laughing. I listen to everyone's prayers. The size or the amount of the requests doesn't matter, I always listen. I love for you to ask me, I love to listen to you speak, don't stop talking to me. I don't need you to lecture me with psalms or hymns repeating them over and over, but rather just talk to me the way you would talk with a friend. After all I am your Father, so let's have a conversation about something or about nothing. Talk to me about how your day went; what you liked about it and what you didn't like. Run your plans by me. Let me be in your life, let me help you decide, let my will be done and you will find out that things are a lot easier when we work together. Learn that I have control over everything and you can avoid many headaches and worries. Don't fear if you stumble today or if you did something that you know you shouldn't; just come to me and we will talk about whatever you want and we can correct anything that needs correcting. The more you come to talk, the easier it will be to start a relationship that grows in love and in faith. You will learn that I never left your side and when you finally decide to come with me with sincerity, you will see that nothing is impossible."

The Church

"All men will hate you because of me, but he who stands firm to the end will be saved."

Matthew 10:22 (NIV)

"Sometimes it's not easy saying the truth, it's not easy admitting that you're wrong, it's not easy to forgive, it's not easy to put up with everything that comes against you but it is a gift that I give you. I require this of you, you can't be like everyone else, you can't be weak in flesh; you have to be strong in spirit. It's not easy; I never said that it wouldn't take dedication to do my will. It's costly. Of course it is, but you are not alone. Many people will curse you because of me, many will treat you unjustly, and many people will hate you on account of me, but stand firm in me, and you will see my power in me and you. The way many people hate you, many will also love you because of me. Many will seek you, and they will invite you over to their house, they will need your guidance. My presence will be so great in your lives that people will not have enough of me by going to church once a week, they will wait everyday outside for the doors to open, they will want to stay there day and night. Miracles will be an everyday experience; the paralyzed will walk, the mute will talk, the blind will see, but most importantly, many will be saved. Many will receive Jesus Christ as their personal savior. People without direction will finally have a goal in their lives. People that were giving up on life will have hope. People that expected nothing from life will have something to live for. You are marching, I have already told you, let my blood cover you, put on your armor, the first step has been taken; now we march."

You Need Faith When You Ask

"Therefore I tell you, whatever you ask for in prayer, believe that you have received it, and it will be yours."

Mark 11:24 (NIV)

9/18/07

"There is something happening in you that cannot be seen, a moving inside of you that cannot be felt, it cannot be smelled but there is a change happening in you whether you feel it or not. Change is slow and sometimes painful but it is necessary. You have to learn how to walk in Spirit so that you could understand that not everything is like it seems and the things that weren't now are. There are things that you don't understand, things that you doubt and you may ask yourself why? Why do you doubt me, is it because you don't understand the way I work? Just because you don't understand doesn't give you an excuse to reason yourself out of not believing. My words are simple but can be complicated, they can be read, but you have to open your eyes, my words can be understood but you have to listen. If you don't listen then how can you understand, you can't understand if you don't walk alongside with me. It's impossible to know me, if you're not with me. You ask for wisdom, yet you just sit around and wait when you should be studying. You ask for a vision but yet you don't pray. You ask of me so many things, and I want to give them to you but you forget what you asked for to begin with.

When you ask, you have to believe in what you're asking for; you have to believe that you will receive it. I listen to every prayer, but remember that it is by faith that you receive all things. Imagine that a child comes and asks you for a toy, you gladly go and buy him the toy to give it to him. When you see this child again, he's asking for another toy, so you put the first toy away and you go and buy him the second toy he asked for. When you see him, he's asking for yet another toy, and he has forgotten and lost all faith in the first two, even though you were about to give it to him. What would you do? Would you give him all three, give him only the first one, or the last one, or would you just wait because you know that tomorrow he will ask for yet another toy. There are so many things that you have asked me for that I was ready to give them to you, but your inconsistency and your lack of faith made me put them away. I am ready to give, if you only believe when you ask."

Your Feelings Are Only the Beginning

He who trusts in himself is a fool, but he who walks in wisdom is kept safe.

Proverbs 28:26 (NIV)

"What did you feel when you were baptized? What did you feel when you received me as your Lord and Savior? I allow you to feel me so that you could be drawn to me. I talk to you through your feelings, but do you have to feel me in order to know that I am there with you? It is easier for you to understand what it is I require of you through emotion. The more you get to know me, the more you will realize that this is only the beginning, and soon those feelings that you were so used to having will be gone. Emotions are beautiful and wonderful, but they are not the primary way in which I use to communicate with you. I am Spirit, and when you feel my presence, it is only because I allow your flesh to feel me, but you cannot rely on them all the time. I am always with you, it is not relevant whether you feel me or not. With time you will see that you don't have to look up in order to hear me, you have to look within you. With time you will realize that sometimes it is difficult to stay afloat in a world of disobedience but the rewards are great. You need to talk with the certainty of faith, you need to walk in Spirit and you need to learn that you are not alone in your decisions. I have control over everything but you must allow me to work. Your feelings turn into faith, and faith is knowing that things happen in your favor whether you feel it or not."

Words

The tongue has the power of life and death, and those who love it will eat its fruit.

Proverbs 18:21 (NIV)

9/19/07

"Learn how to control your emotions, learn how to tame your tongue, and open your ears so that you can listen. Learn to speak only words of encouragement and never argue with those who love to argue. Don't walk in the flesh when you need to walk in the Spirit. Don't let your mind speak its mind, and when you talk from the heart, know that you reveal yourself to others. You will be judged by what you say so be careful in gossiping and understand the power of words. Even a bad joke can have a negative effect on somebody, including yourself. Learn to talk in love and wisdom. Your words create the world around you. Your circumstances are a result of your spoken word. Learn to compliment each other and learn to say 'I love you.' Don't you think it's better to talk in love than to curse? Your words have power for ill or for good, so bless don't curse; lift each other up instead of watching each other fall. Love each other like you would yourself, your words can open doors as well as close them. Let my Holy Spirit guide you in everything you say so that your words can create rather than destroy."

Man

Be self-controlled and alert. Your enemy the devil prowls around like a roaring lion looking for someone to devour.

1 Peter 5:8 (NIV)

9/20/07

"Have you heard how people talk about me? Have you heard their doubts? They are blind with pride; man has always tried to walk his own path without me. Man always wants to have control over everything that surrounds him, can he? With your doubts and your words, you bring sickness into your home. You become sole owners of a disease that doesn't belong to you. You begin to worry, so you take some pills, but why? I am not against science, because I exist everywhere and anywhere. Science can never prove me wrong, but what I am against is your dependency on everything else other than me. You have let the enemy make his home in your heart, maybe you don't feel him, maybe you can't tell the difference, but the moment that you start declaring that you feel sick, you open a door that welcomes disease. The moment that you say that you can't, the enemy is there waiting for your fall. The instant that you give up, the enemy is ready to kick you so you can stay down. You cannot win without me, but with me, you cannot lose. Don't give any room for the enemy; don't let his trickery fool you. Don't doubt the power that I have placed in every one of you, but rather embrace it. Many ask why bad things happen to good people, and they ask me why I permit such things in their lives. But what they don't seem to understand is that sometimes you yourselves open doors that lead to difficulties. The world belongs to the enemy so there is evil all around you. Fret not for you belong to me. You need to submerge yourself completely in my blood. You have to fight if you want to win, let go of any thoughts of negativity, and let me work in your life, in your favor. When things come against you can defend yourself with my Word and my love. A weak mind is controlled rather easily, but a strong mind cannot be broken. Everything that has happened in your life has a purpose but not everything was caused by me."

The Past

"Forget the former things; do not dwell on the past. See, I am doing a new thing! Now it springs up; do you not perceive it? I am making a way in the desert and streams in the wasteland."
Isaiah 43:18–19 (NIV)

9/21/07

"There are so many plans, but so little time. The days seem shorter, and the minutes fly, but the hour still passes at the same time as yesterday. Time runs and never comes back; time doesn't care for mistakes, because they can never be erased. Whatever happened will always be a part of you. The past cannot be changed by the amount of tears that are shed. Even if you ask me, the past will always remain the same. What you can change, however, is your future. You can change the direction in which you were heading; you can change your sinful desires and come and walk along with me. Everyone has something in common, they all have a past. I can help you to leave the past in the past and the arrows of hurt or regret will not bother you anymore. I know you are not perfect, I know you have your faults, and I know your weaknesses, but I still want you. I will guide you one step at a time to rebuild your life, and we will glue it back with love—just like building a puzzle, every piece will be put in its place. Every piece could hurt in the moment that we connect it with others, but it is necessary in order to complete my beautiful work in your life. There is nothing that I cannot do. I can fix anything so don't be afraid of admitting that you are broken."

I Invite You but You Don't Come

"Here I am! I stand at the door and knock. If anyone hears my voice and opens the door, I will come in and eat with him, and he with me."

Revelation 3:20 (NIV)

"Have you seen that it takes dedication to follow me, friends are no more, things that seemed right are now unveiled and you can see their wrong-doing. It has become a struggle to pray and sometimes you get distracted reading my Word. Many things that you were used to are now being shifted and moved to accommodate your new life. Do not conform yourself to this world; you do not belong to it, as you are my children. Everyone is attacked through different angles. The enemy can see your potential, and he doesn't like it. Don't make room in your heart for him. The more often you come and talk to me, the safer you will feel. You must cover yourself with the precious blood of Jesus the Christ. It is no longer a question whether you want to or not come and pray, but rather a necessity that you must do for your own well-being. You cannot sit back and let the enemy rob you of your blessings. The time is short. You have to pray, even if you don't feel like it. That's when you most need it. Don't leave everything for tomorrow, because tomorrow might not come. You have made me a God of 'later,' but when you need my help, you want me to become your God of 'right now.' What would happen if I were to always tell you 'later' rather than 'right now'? You cannot afford to put me last in your life; I have to be the primary reason of your whole being. You were all chosen, because I see what you cannot. I see the potential in your life to be great. Don't go astray from me. I am your King and I am your Shepherd. Don't leave me until 'later.' Let me be at the beginning and at the end of your day. What do you need me to do to show you the importance of coming to my presence every day? You cry out, 'I have no time.' Well then, wake up earlier. You complain that you're tired, that you have to study, that you have to work, but there is no more time for excuses, a soldier of mine has no time for excuses. You want answers to your problems, well then ask me for guidance. You want to be great, well then let me work in you. You want to be healed then all you have to do is kneel and ask me, and I will listen, but I cannot listen to you if you don't ask. I know what it is you are lacking, I know what you are going to ask for before you ask, and I wait for you, waiting to give it to you, but you never come. I wait for you in the car, but you turn up the radio. I wait for you at work, but you are always so busy. I wait for you at night, but you go straight to bed. I wait for you in the kitchen, but you don't want to sit with me and eat. I invite you to come and sit at my table, but you refuse to come. I am the King of kings, and I invite you to break bread with me, but you don't seem to be hungry. I invite you to share a cup of my precious blood, but you are not thirsty. How do you want me to listen if you don't want to sit at my table? How do you want to solve everything if you can't make time to talk? If you don't talk, I can't give what you want.

Do you want miracles to be a part of your life? Do you want people to heal? Do you want your church to grow? Then it's time to put your part. Do you think that because some pray that will be enough? No, everyone has to be in the same page, everyone praying, everyone asking, and everyone on their knees. If you can't make the effort then all you have to do is tell me, and I will find someone to replace you. If you want to be great, then I expect great things from you. Anyone can obey and anyone can listen, so if you don't want to, then all you are doing is taking up the space of someone who is willing. I need workers. I need warriors, I need dedication, and I can't work with someone that bases themselves on what mood they are in today. People that only pray when they have left over time, I cannot use. If you only knew what I have in store for you, the rewards that were waiting for each and every one of you, trust me, motivation would not be an issue. I love you, and I am with you, Jesus of Nazareth."

The Complaint

Be joyful always; pray continually; give thanks in all circumstances, for this is God's will for you in Christ Jesus.

1 Thessalonians 5:16–18 (NIV)

9/22/07

"How many complaints do you have against each other? You complain about everything. 'Why is this like that? How come so early? Why? Why?' You complain so much that you forget what it was that you were complaining about. You have to learn to see the positive side in everything, learn to open your eyes with love. It's difficult at first, but you can change your perspective and you will be able to change your complaints into gratefulness. Take my hand. You have to learn to be grateful no matter what happens. Nothing happens without my will when we walk together. So in reality when you are always complaining; you are complaining about me and what I do. A student cannot complain of what the teacher is teaching him, unfortunately that's the way you have made it, you complain without seeing the final outcome. And when you finally see the final result, you don't know where to hide your shame after everything turned out fine. A complaint damages oneself primarily, negative thoughts creep in and the negativity starts to become your way of life and you will be unable to see the good in everything and start to criticize. It is not good to criticize with malicious intent. It's not good to make fun of someone to hurt them. Learn how to be compassionate and loving. Just the way it is easy to find the bad in anyone, it is even easier to find the good. Just the way you work hard to make someone feel bad, work twice as hard to make someone feel good. Just the way you can be ungrateful, you can always be thankful. Treat your brother as you would yourself."

The Purpose

In him we were also chosen, having been predestined according to the plan of him who works out everything in conformity with the purpose of his will, in order that we, who were first to hope in Christ, might be for the praise of his glory.

Ephesians 1:11–12 (NIV)

9/23/07

"What do you think is God's purpose in your life? What is the plan? Let's analyze this. First: What do you think? Do you even believe? Do you have faith in what God has told you, do you believe without a doubt when God speaks? Second: Purpose. Everyone has a purpose whether you understand it or not. Everyone has a destiny that can only develop living in Spirit through your choices. Your destiny cannot be guided by your flesh; it has to be guided by the Spirit. This is the only way your pre-destiny to become like Jesus can be accomplished. Third: God. The plans for your life all come from God, they have never been of your doing, there is no way you can know what is better for you, God knows everything. Learn to trust your ways to God and you will learn to rest on him. Fourth: Your life. I didn't ask you about everyone else's life, but I asked you about your own life. Every single one of you is special to me; I made each of you in my image before you were in your mother's womb. Your life in this world is not just to survive but to live, it is to come to me and help me spread my Word; it is to be in communion with me. Every life has the same pre-destiny to come back home to their Creator but some decide to go another route. Others think that their way is better but one day you will realize that in order to walk towards me, you're going to have to let go of some of the things that hold you back. Come to my path of life."

The Tree

"'This is what you are to say to Joseph: I ask you to forgive your brothers the sins and the wrongs they committed in treating you so badly.' Now please forgive the sins of the servants of the God of your father." When their message came to him, Joseph wept.

Genesis 50:17 (NIV)

9/23/07

"You have to learn how to forgive, you have to learn to really forgive from the inside out, let go of all pride and forgive from the heart. Don't forgive just with your words. Dig deep into your heart and pull out that root of resentment and anger, then you will be truly free. Many can ask for forgiveness and many can forgive with their mouths but empty words can be swept away by the wind. Kneel and pull out that weed in your life; even though it hurts it must be done. Burn every bridge that leads to rage, resentment and pride. When you get rid of all the roots, when you forgive, then you will have an empty space in your soul and many make the mistake of leaving that space empty. You have to plant love. You have to plant wisdom and obedience so that the weed of an unforgiving heart will not be able to grow again in that place. You can water love and obedience with your thoughts, with your words, with your actions, and they will grow and produce good fruit. The weeds also need to be watered, but you must choose to water only one, and the more you water one, the more it will consume the other until the waterless withers and dies. Learn to water the tree of life, because I Am is the water of life and not of death. If you continue to water the tree of death, then it will grow, and it will consume you, it will be more difficult to dig around the trunk and pull it from its roots. But if you water the tree of life by praying, by repenting, by forgiving, by reading my Word, thinking and acting positive and speaking words of encouragement, then the tree of life will grow and give off beautiful fruit that everyone around you can enjoy. People can eat of the fruit that you produce, and they will spit out their seeds back at you. You have a decision every day of your life, which tree will you water today?"

Growing

When I was a child, I talked like a child, I thought like a child, I reasoned like a child. When I became a man, I put childish ways behind me.

1 Corinthians 13:11 (NIV)

9/24/07

"There are so many questions and so few answers. There are so many doubts but little confirmations of truth. What is happening? You feel alone but you're not. You feel your prayers aren't heard but they are. Are they tests? Are these attacks from the enemy? What is happening is that you are growing in faith, you are growing as a Christian, you are going from crawling to walking and things need to change. The more you learn to depend on me, the more responsibility you will have. With every step that is taken, things begin to change for the better. The more you realize that I am always with you, the more you will realize that you don't need to feel me to know that I am here with you. You will know that feelings cannot be depended upon. It is difficult to grow, change is not easy, but it is necessary if you want more from me. I have to wash all your impurities; I must clean the stain of sin in your life. I always listen, I am always there, you are never alone, and I am always by your side guiding you. Learn to quiet yourself so that you can listen to me."

The Harvest

"Give, and it will be given to you. A good measure, pressed down, shaken together and running over, will be poured into your lap. For with the measure you use, it will be measured to you."

Luke 6:38 (NIV)

9/25/07

"The more you give the more I give you. I love the cheerful giver, and I love it when my children come to me giving with joy. The rewards for giving are vast and beneficial to your soul. The more you give the more your room is filled with treasures, the most beautiful diamond here on earth cannot even begin to compare to what I have here for everyone who gives cheerfully. You reap what you sow. You sow love you will reap love. If you sow patience you will reap patience; everything has a reward. The negative seeds that are sowed have a consequence, that's why you have to be careful of what you sow, because you will reap it sooner or later. Don't give just for the rewards, give with a pure heart and without the stain of greed; give without sadness or obligation, and give because you want to give. Motivation is the key to giving cheerfully and receiving blissfully. My children are always willing to give; they want more so that they can give more. I give to those who want to give, I give to those who are unselfish and I thank you for sharing what I give you. In the end, everything will fade away, but the fruit of the Spirit will never pass away. It is important to sow things of the Spirit, love, patience, time, faith, because this and many more seeds will bring joy to your soul, all this that you sow will bring happiness in your life. Sow for the Kingdom."

A Little about Heaven

But in keeping with his promise we are looking forward to a
new heaven and a new earth, the home of righteousness.

2Peter 3:13 (NIV)

9/27/07

"How do you imagine heaven is like? I have showed you already
but there is so much that is yet to be seen. The New Jerusalem is an
immense beautiful city. It is filled with love and splendor. It is not a
small town but a city paved with gold. There are green pastures, riv-
ers, and it is never dark. My glory is always shimmering. There are
mountains all around, flowers that seem like crystals, gardens; there
is so much happiness here. There is so much joy that it cannot be
contained. There are feasts, food, entertainment, but most of all, I am
here, walking amongst you, and they love me and hug me as I hug
them. There is worship, there are angels walking and working. There
are buildings made of gold and precious stones, there is water clear as
crystal, and if you want you can swim in it. There is no sadness, there
is no fear, and there is no death. You can imagine the rewards that I
have for each worker but still your mind cannot perceive. With time I
will show you more, but for now, it is enough. If you were to see it all
at once, you would not want to go back to earth."

Speaking with Action

In the same way, faith by itself, if it is not accompanied by action, is dead.

James 2:17 (NIV)

"You have to learn how to bring people to me, talk about my kingdom, about my love, but you also have to learn how to act like my children. Words have power, but they also have to be backed up by action. A word without any form of action is dead, a spoken word that is not practiced is of no worth, a Christian that talks but does not act according to what he says would be better if he would stay quiet. If you're going to talk then be ready to act, and if you're going to act then be ready to speak. People will ask you what has happened to you. They will ask you why you are so happy. This is your cue, a perfect opportunity to let them know what kind of God you serve. If you only say, 'I don't know,' then it would be as if you are denying me because you know why you have changed but yet you give me no glory. Are you ashamed? Be it what it is, you can proclaim my love for you to others. Jesus spoke but he also acted, his actions backed up his words and his words backed up his actions. His words would have been void if his actions did not prove what he said, his resurrection for instance. You have the capacity to teach people what you are made of when it all seems to come against you. In the circumstances, in weakness, let your actions be caressed by your words. What benefit is there to behave upright when everything is going great; the secret is to act upright when everything seems to be wrong. Patience is not acquired when everything seems to be in control. The secret does not lie in the situation but your behavior in the situation. The secret does not lie in the complaining but rather in staying quiet when you disagree in something. The situation will not change by the amount of your complaining, it's your attitude that needs to change and you will see a solution. Back up your positive words with affirmative action."

Learn

Blessed is the man who finds wisdom, the man who gains understanding,

Proverbs 3:13 (NIV)

9/29/07

"You have to be able to endure criticism to be my servant. You will be the center of attacks, but you will trust me, and you will know that you are free from any curse that comes against you. A servant never stops growing, never stops learning. You can spend your whole life trying to understand me, but I tell you now that it will not be enough time. I will show you what I need to show you, the Holy Spirit will guide you and open your eyes; you will see things that weren't there before, but in reality, they were always present. It's just that you were blind. But how do you want me to show you if you don't open your Bible? You have to put your part as well, learn to pass your time with me so that I can show you my secrets. The more time you spend with me, the more you will understand my purpose in your life. Everything is so simple, but you make it complicated. Everything is written but hidden, everything is said, but there is no one to listen. Set time to learn, set time to read. Some want to learn everything, but they don't know anything. Some want to understand everything, but they just sit there and wait for a lighting bolt to hit them with all the answers. Learn to set apart time for me and I will set apart time for you. Ask for wisdom and I will give it to you."

The Blind, Mute, Deaf

"Not everyone who says to me, 'LORD, LORD,' will enter the kingdom of heaven, but only he who does the will of my Father who is in heaven. Many will say to me on that day, 'LORD, LORD, did we not prophesy in your name, and in your name drive out demons and perform many miracles?' Then I will tell them plainly, 'I never knew you. Away from me, you evildoers!'"

Matthew 7:21–23 (NIV)

"The blind thinks that he can see, the mute thinks that he knows what to say, and the deaf thinks that he knows how to listen. But I tell you, the blind cannot see, the mute doesn't talk, and the deaf doesn't hear. There are many that believe they have me in their hearts, there are people that just sit back comfortably and deceive themselves thinking that they are going to heaven. The blind only sees what he wants, only what is to his benefit and liking. He doesn't see his errors or his weaknesses; he doesn't see that he is walking blindly following the wrong path. He tries to teach others and leads them to death. He thinks his life is complete, but it is lacking. He speaks of heaven and of hell, but he doesn't worry. He is like the servant that fell asleep waiting for his master. He is like a light that only shines when in company, but when he is alone, it is dark. The mute always believes he is right; he thinks he knows everything there is to know about me. If you try to explain something to him, he will just interrupt you with his own conclusions. In reality, he is stubborn and selfish. He is not open to any new ideas; he is close-minded and doesn't accept anything that doesn't coincide with his beliefs. In his selfishness, he is trapped in his own little world of ideas, and when he prays, all he asks for is for everyone else to change instead of asking for a change for himself. The mute needs to learn how to be quiet and understand that he isn't always right. The deaf listens only to what he wants to hear and still doesn't pay attention. He comes to me only in necessity, and when I help him, he forgets about me. He comes crying and begging, but like I said, as soon as I show him the way, he forgets to thank me and even believes that it was all his doing. He doesn't like to hear that he is wrong, he only wants to hear pleasant things from me. He gets offended when you try to correct him. He is a fool that cannot be saved, because he only looked for me in selfishness, only in his need, and never because he loved me. He searched and found me, and then forgot me. When I come, the mute will tell me, 'I talked about you,' and I will say, 'You talked about yourself, and sometimes included me, I do not know you.' The blind will say, 'I showed everyone the way Lord,' and I will say, 'You never showed yourself the way. I don't know you.' The deaf will tell me, 'I came to you Lord and heard what you said,' and I will say, 'You never listened, and I waited for you every day, and still you did not come.' My way is easy, but you can make it difficult. My way cannot be walked by the flesh alone; my way is always lit, but still some struggle to see."

Just Come

Therefore, brothers, since we have confidence to enter the Most Holy Place by the blood of Jesus, by a new and living way opened for us through the curtain, that is, his body, and since we have a great priest over the house of God, let us draw near to God with a sincere heart in full assurance of faith, having our hearts sprinkled to cleanse us from a guilty conscience and having our bodies washed with pure water.

Hebrews 10:19–22 (NIV)

9/30/07

"You have to stop listening to your flesh and come to me in Spirit. Let your past sins go and simply come. You have to learn to trust that I take care of you and nothing bad is going to happen to you. Don't be afraid of being imperfect, don't be afraid of being perfect, and don't be afraid to fall. I am not a God of dread but a God of love. With love, obedience follows, but first come to me and we will work together in washing away your impurities in your life. It's a trap that many people fall into when they think I don't want them to come because of their sins. People stay away because they are afraid of change. This is a deception of the enemy, because I came for the sinners. I came for everyone, for everyone needs me. If someone is afraid of coming to pray because they are sinners, then they will remain sinners, because they never came and therefore still live in the flesh. I understand that you can't be perfect, I can't expect you to be perfect because you can't, the only way to purify yourselves is through me, everyday, every night, every morning. If you don't come, you will just be left wanting; if you don't come you will only watch me from afar but never know me. If you don't come your dread will consume you, and you will find out too late that your only way to be free was through me. You will spend your life trying to change something that you can't change by yourself. You will wait for a miracle, but you will never take a step forward. You will spend your life wishing, but your wishes cannot be heard if you don't come and speak with me. I know what is in your heart, even before you ask, I know. Don't try to hide, I already know everything, and anything you try to hide, I find. I only ask you to come and talk with me everyday, and you will see that everything else will fall into place with time. I am in control. Jesus of Nazareth."

Part III: October

The Commandments

And now , O Israel, what does the LORD your God ask of you but to fear the LORD your God, to walk in all his ways, to love him, to serve the LORD your God with all your heart and with all your soul, and to observe the LORD's commands and decrees that I am giving you today for your own good?

Deuteronomy 10:12–13 (NIV)

10/01/07

"Do you think that one day your actions will justify your wrongdoings? Do you think you can do one good deed and then turn around and commit two bad ones? Do you think there is a balance when you say, 'Well I did my good deed for today, now it doesn't really matter what I do for the rest of the day.' Do you think one is less or more of a sinner if he is caught in adultery or commits murder? I have said that if you break one command, then you break all of them. If you disobey one then you disobey in all of them. Then what are you to do? Someone who doesn't honor his or her parents is the same as one who has other gods before me. Is adultery the same as a thief that is spending his time in jail? Yes. The commandments weren't written so that you can follow some of them, all of them were meant to be followed. I am not a God of sometimes, and if you disobey one then you disobey them all. Two rights cannot cover one wrong, you would be mistaken if you thought this. All your good can never cover one bad, you can't steal and be free from the rest of them. A sinner is a sinner, if this wasn't the case then all I had to say was to follow whichever command fits you best, and if you can't with one, at least try to follow the rest. Your flesh cannot follow all of my laws; it is too weak to obey by itself. It is impossible for man to follow all of my wishes, all of my laws, all of my commandments. Then how? You have to die and let go of all your fears and your flesh will die. You must be born again into a new life. Without Jesus you can do nothing, let the Holy Spirit guide you. He has to abide in you; it is the only way to follow me. Is it a trap? No, but a reality that by yourself you cannot keep them all because you will fall into the desires of the flesh. The only way to be in perfection is to be guided by the Spirit. Man cannot save himself or make himself righteous; righteousness and salvation came through the Christ. Come, I will give you the bread that takes away hunger. Come, I will give you the wine that takes away all thirst. Eat my body and drink my blood and you will have eternal life."

Fear

But be sure to fear the LORD and serve him faithfully with all your heart; consider what great things he has done for you.

1 Samuel 12:24 (NIV)

10/02/07

"How can you defeat fear? You have to stand up to it but not by yourself, you have to stand on the rock that is me so that you can fight it. It is not easy because everyone has fears, whether they be physical or emotional, financial, or psychological. Fears or phobias do not come from me. The only fear I require is the reverence of me for those who know me and dread from those who oppose me. I am not a God that puts a spirit fear in people's lives. The first step in defeating fear is admitting that you fear, don't be deceived by the enemy and don't let pride stand in your way. The second is coming to me and pray diligently so that fear won't be a part of you anymore, and soon the fear will disappear. The third is to die to your fleshy desires and let the Holy Spirit guide you in all truth. The Spirit will reveal to you the hidden fears you didn't know you had. Your flesh is fearing, but your Spirit is not. Don't be fooled into thinking that there is no cure, because I tell you that through Jesus, everyone is already free. Don't fear anyone except me."

Change Hurts

And we know that in all things God works for the good of those who love him, who have been called according to his purpose. For those God foreknew he also predestined to be conformed to the likeness of his Son, that he might be the firstborn among many brothers.

Romans 8:28–29 (NIV)

10/3/07

"When you ask for change, you expect one day to wake up and automatically be transformed, walking in love, in wisdom, with joy, but in reality that change takes work. It's difficult because of the tendencies of the flesh that manipulates your reaction in a certain situation. It manipulates you so much that it eventually becomes a part of you and you believe that it is part of your personality. But it is not. If you would open your eyes and read my Word, you will find out that rage, gossiping, vanity, pride, and many more are not from me, and they don't belong to you either. Change hurts, you will have to sustain your tongue from saying things that are not productive, but you will also learn to say things that you don't want to say that are loving and caring. You are not alone; I am with you in every area of your life that you want to improve. But why do you have to wait until you want to change in order to change? I don't force change on anybody but it is necessary. Surrender your will to me and let my will be done in your life. The only person standing in your way is you. Change is necessary if you want to be like Christ. Sanctification is a lifetime process with eternal rewards."

The Way

By day the LORD went ahead of them in a pillar of cloud to guide them on their way and by night in a pillar of fire to give them light, so that they could travel by day or night. Neither the pillar of cloud by day nor the pillar of fire by night left its place in front of the people.

Exodus 13:21–22 (NIV)

"You come to pray, but it seems like if no one is listening. Your day passes, and you feel alone. You speak but your words seem dry. What is going on? You're walking through a desert; your faithfulness is being tested. Do you come and pray just because it made you feel good or because you wanted to spend time with your Father? If you came to me just for reasons of your selfishness, meaning that you only prayed in order to feel good; then what is going to happen when your feelings deceive you and you feel nothing? You will feel like if prayer was a waste of time. Will you die in the desert or will you fight against your self and understand that I will slowly change what I have to change in you and reveal myself to you. There are children of mine that walk around the same mountain for years, because they don't open themselves up to what I am trying to show them. Being a Christian is not about only receiving but of giving. Give your time, give your love, but don't expect something in return. Don't expect your prayers to always be full of feelings, because I can't base myself on that. You don't need to feel me in order to know that I am always there. In your little faith, you stop praying because you think since you don't feel me then obviously I left you by yourself. Some want me to perform miracles in front of them; they want the skies to open and my voice be heard in order for them to listen. Some of you want immediate answers to your prayers, and still others test me and tell me, 'If you only heal me then I will know that it is you who is working in my life.' Why? Why do you need so much proof of my existence? Isn't faith believing in things even though you don't see them? You don't need to remind me of what I need to do for you like if I have to do them. I told you once what I wanted from you, an obedient son that I don't have to be repeating myself on what I want from him. I want to ask only once, why do I have to ask it of you many times? You don't have to come to me and say 'What do I do.' Rather come to me and say, 'Father, I know what I have to do, help me and guide me so that your will be done and not mine, so that your wisdom flows through me, and I can discern what is yours and what is not, shine away all evil and deceit from the enemy. Thank you for my daily bread. Thank you because you are in control, and I know that whatever happens in my life is of no surprise to you, thank you for opening my eyes to see the things you want me to see. Thank you for opening my ears so I am able to hear your voice and listen to your whispers. Thank you for blessing my tongue so that I can bless and not curse. Thank you because as long as I am with you, I will lack nothing. The blood of Christ covers me and protects me, thank you for the fruit that flows out of your joy and that the people around me can benefit from what you give me, because they will know that I am not alone, but that you are with me Lord. Then people will ask me where the ray of sunshine is coming from, and I will give you all praise and glory my God, because you have given me the ability to talk about your kingdom and of your power and love.' What I say is, don't walk around the same mountain, take some time to listen to what I have to say. Don't walk in vain, just open your eyes and see the path that lies ahead."

The Future

But those who hope in the LORD will renew their strength. They will soar on wings like eagles; they will run and not grow weary, they will walk and not be faint.

Isaiah 40:31 (NIV)

10/04/07

"If you could see your future, do you think that your prayers would change in the present? If you could see the things you ask for and understand that I don't give them to you because I have something better for you, would you keep on insisting for the same thing? It would make your life easier if I could reveal the future to you, future in respect as to what it is you pray for. Someone could be praying for a certain job, but they don't see the hindrances that job will bring, so I wait in answering your prayer, because I see that it will only bring you temporary satisfaction. I always have something better, so don't get upset when you don't get what you asked for. I am working for your benefit, and I am cleaning everything that needs to be cleansed in you. Some changes are difficult but necessary if you want to continue along the lighted path. I am always your friend and it doesn't matter what you did or where you came from; I will always be there but you have a choice if you want to befriend me or not. Don't let the enemy deceive you into thinking that you are alone, don't let the enemy torture you with lies. Beyond the lie, there is deception, a deception that you alone fell into by believing the lies. But even if you fall in them, that shouldn't stop you from praying. On the contrary, that should motivate you into praying more, because you will find out that you can't do it by yourself. Surrender your life to me, keep on praying, and you will see changes in your life—changes that maybe you won't see right away but slowly they will reveal themselves. Don't lose faith, and don't lose hope, because everything is already done, you just need to take it."

Time and Love

But the fruit of the Spirit is love, joy, peace, patience, kindness, goodness, faithfulness, gentleness and self-control. Against such things there is no law.

Galatians 5:22–23 (NIV)

"What is the best thing that you can give me? Time, which is short, so you need to take advantage of it by coming to me everyday and let me guide you wherever you go. Is it too much to ask? Your time. What can you offer me that has no price? Love, which is wrapped around with obedience, joy, patience, and everything beautiful but true love comes from loving your Father that gives and takes care of you. Invest your time to know me, and you will be able to see the love that flows in the world. Time and love need each other, they draw from each other, if you don't love me then what good is your time and if you don't have time for me, how can you love me? Love that stands still, of what use is it? Time that is stagnant is just wasting away. I give you time so that you can dedicate it to me and my work, and I gave you love so you can benefit by giving and receiving from it in the short time that you are here. Love to do my will. Jesus of Nazareth."

The Washing of Feet

But I tell you: Love your enemies and pray for those who persecute you, that you may be sons of your Father in heaven. He causes his sun to rise on the evil and the good, and sends rain on the righteous and the unrighteous.

Matthew 5:44–45 (NIV)

10/5/07

"Love your enemies as you love yourself. Do for them what you want people to do for you. Your enemy will turn into your friend when he sees that you love him amidst everything. When I washed the feet of my disciples, Judas was among them. I knew that he would betray me, but yet I still washed his feet, because I loved him as well. Could you have done the same? Love is not just receiving but giving and not just giving, but giving it to those that don't seem to deserve it. There is the real test, in loving those who hate you, you can become more and more like me. What reward is there in loving only those who love you, in doing a favor and then expecting payment, helping those that help you? There's a test of true love, to help someone that has never helped you; there is more companionship when someone who speaks ill of you asks you to pray for him. My children cannot help only those that help them in return. Help those that don't ask; help my lost sheep. The world will hate you, but your love will transcend the darkness. You must wash everyone's feet, even if you know that they will betray you."

A Good Friend

I pray that you may be active in sharing your faith, so that you will have a full understanding of every good thing we have in Christ.

Philemon 1:6 (NIV)

10/6/07

"Don't be afraid of telling people that I guide your steps, don't be afraid of teaching them how I am a part of your life, and don't be afraid of saying something inappropriate, because I will speak for you. There is so much that you have yet to learn, and within time, I will show you more and more, and you will be able to answer anyone's questions with ease. People will be amazed at the answers that you will give them. They will know that it is I who is speaking through you, and they will listen attentively. There isn't much to say when your actions reveal my glory and you live by what you teach. Learn to listen so that you can see the hearts of the people that come your way. Listening is just as important as talking; you will soon find out that the more you listen the more you will be able to talk about things that matter to them. My disciples and I spend sleepless nights just talking and listening. We laughed, talked, joked, sang, and our relationships grew in love the more time we would spend together. To talk about me and my Father you don't have to be in church, you don't have to be in class, you can talk about me with your friends, brothers, strangers in any place and any time. Don't worry about other people's sin, focus on their salvation, introduce them to me, teach them that I love the sinner and they will slowly learn how I love them despite their shortcomings. Your loved ones will entertain many. It is no coincidence that you run into someone; I put everyone in your path. They will look for you, and your friends will increase. A warrior of mine is friendly and loving, and a warrior spends time with everyone and lets my light shine the way. With your love you attract people to me. Those who are in darkness look for the light, whether they know it or not. They search without knowing what they are searching for, and they will find me. They find out that it was I who was missing in their lives. Just let me guide you in everything and all the things that seemed unfair will turn out even better than you thought, just let me talk and they will listen, don't worry about changing someone's mind but rather let me work in them. Don't let it bother you that they talk bad about me, I can protect myself. Occupy yourself just by talking about me and planting the seed; I will make it grow. How can you begin to plant it? By being a good friend. Would you give your life for them? I did, and not just for my friends but for my enemies. A friend forgives and forgets, a friend loves, and never rejects; a friend listens and doesn't talk ill of others. Do you think I was a good friend? Do you think my followers were good friends? They hid, they ran away, they denied me, rejected me, betrayed me, and left me alone, but even then I still love them with all my heart. A good friend is always looking for ways to forgive those who hurt him. If Judas would have asked for forgiveness, I was more than willing to give it to him. I was waiting for him, but his own condemnation brought him to his end. I wept for him because I love him just as I weep for all those that deny me. Love between friends grows. In the end, we are all brothers and sisters of Jesus, children of God, and friends of the Holy Spirit."

Do Good

Our people must learn to devote themselves to doing what is good, in order that they may provide for daily necessities and not live unproductive lives.

Titus 3:14 (NIV)

10/7/07

"A worker rejoices in doing my will, he doesn't just do what I ask but he enjoys doing what I ask. He enjoys serving his King, because he knows that he is well taken care of. If you are to help someone, help them with a willing attitude. If they ask for help, then out of the good of your heart, help. You are at risk of losing all the blessings I had for you when you start complaining for helping. This doesn't mean that you always have to say 'yes' when they ask, but it does mean that when you do agree to help, to help out of love. When you help those who need help, you are doing my will, you don't necessarily have to talk just about me, but a simple conversation with someone that has no one to talk to, or giving someone a ride to work, all these things even though they don't seem godly, in reality they are. I reside in love; I am in every one of you, and I help you to want to do good every day. Don't think that I only work when you are at church, you are the church, and I am working through you. Don't think that because you don't know all the scriptures you can't help someone understand. All those who work out of love are doing my will. But you also have to understand that you have to come to me;

doing good is only the beginning, come to my presence everyday and let Jesus be your King so that your soul will be saved from destruction. Doing good is part of being my child but only the beginning for many."

Trust Him

"For I know the plans I have for you," declares the LORD, "plans to prosper you and not to harm you, plans to give you hope and a future. Then you will call upon me and come and pray to me, and I will listen to you. You will seek me and find me when you seek me with all your heart."

Jeremiah 29:11–13 (NIV)

10/08/07

"Not only do you have to depend on me, you also have to trust me. To depend is leaving all your worries and troubles, your finances, your doubts, your problems, and bringing them and leaving them here with me. You come to a point when you realize that you can't make it on your own and hence, you need a rock that you can stand on. You need to trust me after you depend on me. Do you trust that everything that you bring to me will be taken care of? There are many that come and leave their worries and troubles, but yet when they leave they don't trust that I can handle them. With your mouth you confess that God is in control, but you don't trust me. In the moment that something unexpected happens, you come to me and complain—you complain because that wasn't in your agenda. You don't trust the Father that feeds you. You don't trust the Father that takes care of you. You can try to depend on me, but it will seem impossible if you don't trust me. Open the door to your house and let me live among you, once you leave your worries to me, you must learn to walk away and trust that I know what I am doing. Everything is not always going to turn out the way you want it to happen but rather how I need it to happen. Everything always works out for the good of your soul, even though sometimes it doesn't seem like it. I can turn water into wine, darkness into light, sadness into love. After you trust me then depend on me, after you depend on me you will learn to have faith in what I do, and your faith will begin to increase, your love will show, and your insecurities will be washed away, because you will know that I watch over my children. Come to me and leave your troubles, but trust me with them as well. Don't come to me uncertain of my power and then expect me to work everything out. Learn that everything you bring to me I will help you with. I know what is best for you, whether you see it or not."

I

A man of many companions may come to ruin, but there is a friend who sticks closer than a brother.

Proverbs 18:24 (NIV)

10/9/07

"Maybe you haven't made time to appreciate today, maybe you haven't finished what you needed to do, or maybe you don't understand why certain things happen to you. I walk next to you in everything that you do, even in the simplest of things I am there. Even if they seem boring to you, I am still by your side. I walk with you when you get upset and when you're full of joy; I walk in front of you when you are scared and when you are brave. I walk beside you when you are uncertain of your future or reflect on your past, and I walk along with you when you are hurt as well as when you laugh. I watch you when you sleep and when you run; I listen when you talk and when you're quiet; I take your hand only when you ask, and I carry you when you are tired. I protect you from anything bad happening to you, and I bless you with everything good. I talk with you in the mornings, and I wait for you in the evenings. I exercise with you, and I also rest alongside you. I am there with you, even when the days are spontaneous or planned. I always take your love and multiply it; I always hold on to your smile and I plant a seed with it; I dance when you dance or sit when you rather sit. I am always with you."

Calmness

Do not be anxious about anything, but in everything, by prayer
and petition, with thanksgiving, present your requests to God.
And the peace of God, which transcends all understanding, will
guard your hearts and your minds in Christ Jesus.

Philippians 4:6–7 (NIV)

10/11/07

"Sometimes you need to calm your flesh in order to calm your soul.
During the day one is always in a hurry trying to finish everything
fast and when you are done, you only find that you have other things
to do. Don't bring your hurriedness when you pray. Take your time
and rest your flesh so that your soul can benefit. Simply come and
rest with me, you don't have to talk, just listen. Close your eyes,
breathe, and listen to yourself. Your day will pass through your mind
and just let all that filter out. Your impatience will grow impatient
and you will find patience. Forget everything and concentrate on my
love, let me hug you and your worries will not be a burden to you
anymore. Your troubles are not who you are but rather just some
dust that must be wiped off. Rest your flesh, your mind will follow
then your soul and then the Spirit will shine through you. True peace
comes from the inside out. I have control over everything and anything. I take care of you, say it, believe it, and don't doubt. Because
everything that happens when we're together I let it happen, and I
always use the experience for your benefit. But understand that I am
not a God who sends down evil to you. Evil is caused by man and
the enemy. So, when you begin to rest in me then we can begin to

talk, then your soul is more apt to listening to what I have to tell you. I love it when you seek me just to talk, it doesn't have to be all about me but rather things about you as well. How was your day? Why were you upset? Who won? In reality, it can be anything as long as I get to talk to you as your Father. I love you and take care of you. Your heavenly Father."

The World

"Come to me, all you who are weary and burdened, and I will give you rest. Take my yoke upon you and learn from me, for I am gentle and humble in heart, and you will find rest for your souls. For my yoke is easy and my burden is light."

Matthew 11:28–30 (NIV)

10/12/07

"Imagine a world where evil would not exist, where everything would be done out of love and for love, and where tears are only for joy and worry is replaced by trust. Imagine a place where money is of no value but rather your actions and reactions would be the currency, a place where you can take time off to rest and breathe. Don't be so anxious in reaching heaven, don't frustrate yourself with things in this world, and don't you realize that you don't have to come looking for me when I am already in you. You can have peace here, but you must learn to rest in me, let me take your worries. I am the light in the darkness, and I am your guide in your path that sometimes seems obscured with doubt. I carry you when you tire, I wait when you need to rest and talk, and I look for you when you seem lost. Don't let this world mistreat you. I made you to conquer it, not for it to conquer you. Don't conform yourself to it but rather let the world change because of you. Appreciate every day, seize it, because time runs in a hurry and doesn't rest. The world can be cruel if you let it, and the world can deceive you if you're not careful. I created the world for you, but you must also learn to live through me in it. I have control over every leave that moves. Nothing happens without my consent, but don't trust the world—trust me, the Creator. Don't depend on your strengths but in mine, and don't try to control everything, because you'll end up losing control. Don't try to please everyone, because you'll only aggravate them. Your will cannot be done if you abide in me and I in you."

Follow

"The man who loves his life will lose it, while the man who hates his life in this world will keep it for eternal life. Whoever serves me must follow me; and where I am, my servant also will be. My Father will honor the one who serves me."

John 12:25–26 (NIV)

"In order to truly follow me, you have to learn to sacrifice certain things, you have to learn to put my will before yours. I have freed you from the chains of oppression. You can run and go anywhere you please but not every place brings you bliss. You can't be guided by feelings but by trusting me with your obedience. I can't guide someone who wants to do only what they want, I can't help someone who doesn't want to help themselves when they don't feel like praying. If you are willing to change, then I am willing to change you. I need you to listen to what I have to say. Produce fruit that is edible by everyone. I leave you my Spirit and yet you still doubt. The Spirit of truth has power but you have to put that power to practice, don't worry about the details in life, I always have something better than what you can see. We are marching and fighting together. Don't fear and don't doubt."

Question

For wisdom will enter your heart, and knowledge will be pleasant to your soul.

Proverbs 2:10 (NIV)

10/13/07

"Don't feel like a fool when you realize that all you've learned is really just the surface of things. One lifetime is not enough time to learn everything that needs to be learned. You will have all eternity to comprehend whatever it is you want to learn about. In the meantime, I will show you what I need you to learn so that you won't waste your time on something that is not beneficial. If you are thirsty, I will give you something to drink. Seek wisdom and knowledge not just for your benefit but for the benefit of others. Wisdom is the answer to all your questions. I like it when someone wants to know me, because wisdom is worth more than gold and silver. Ask me, and I will guide you in all truths. Don't be impatient when it seems that I don't answer; it's just that sometimes the answer is right in front of you, and all you have to do is open your eyes. If you ask the Father in my name, it will be given to you. So why don't you simply ask when you're in doubt? If one refrains from asking, everything can seem confusing, but the Spirit knows everything. There isn't a question that is too difficult to answer but don't spend too much time on one, because there is much to learn and so little time. Take time to learn things that will help you grow as well as the kingdom.

But you have to spend time with me so that I can reveal to you the secrets hidden in plain sight. The same way I spoke with Abraham, I can talk with you—in a relationship of true friendship, without fear, and with a boasting confidence. Friends are always there to help through the doubts."

Obedience

As Jesus went on from there, he saw a man named Matthew sitting at the tax collector's booth. "Follow me," he told him, and Matthew got up and followed him.

Matthew 9:9 (NIV)

10/14/07

"It's difficult obeying when you don't understand why you have to do it. It's difficult obeying when you're accustomed to doing what you want. Obedience is not learned, obedience is not read. Obedience is only accomplished through practice. You have to learn to obey with the small tasks so that you can be trusted with bigger tasks. Don't try to run when you're barely learning to crawl; I will know when you are ready to receive more responsibility. Learn to sacrifice your self-centeredness and have compassion of everyone around you. In order to be the best, you have to be the last; an obedient heart brings joy to the Father, because he will know that you are willing to do his will. It is a battle that must be fought between your ego and your love, you will have to let go of your desires and your plans and let God be God in your life. Surrender so that you will die to your old ways, only so that you can live. Many come but fear the change that must be made in their lives, so they just come and talk. Then they leave abruptly before I begin to speak. A true friend makes time to be with me, he gives me his life, his time, he puts his desires second, and he lets my will be done. Learn to obey what I say, because I always have a better plan for you. Obeying is not only when it seems beneficial but also when you don't know the outcome—that is complete trust in what I say. It will cost you pride, and it will take some time, because the worst enemy of disobedience is oneself. You deceive yourself and even talk yourself into doing things that are not my will, and you wait for another sign even when I have already told you what I need you to do. Sometimes you wait to see if I changed my mind and tell you something like, 'You were right.' But that will never happen, because man will never know more than God. I am always right, even when you don't understand how. Just obey and you will see that everything is under my control, everything always comes out according to plan, as long as you do my will. Don't draw your own conclusions; I always have something better and besides I am the only one that knows how this could end. Don't argue with me, because in the end, I am trying to help you. Don't test me, because disobeying is not an option. How else can you serve me? Surrender yourself and trust in what I do in your life."

Three

"But the Counselor, the Holy Spirit, whom the Father will send in my name, will teach you all things and will remind you of everything I have said to you."

John 14:26 (NIV)

10/15/07

"It is important for you to remember that you have to ask everything in the name of Jesus. You cannot reach the Father if you don't go through the Son first. Jesus is salvation, and he is the only path there is to take. Without the Son, your communication with the Father would be void and empty. Without the Holy Spirit, you would not be able to communicate through Jesus. We are three, but we are also one. It is difficult to understand, because as we are one; we also have our own distinct personalities. How then can you find out who it is you are talking to? You can talk to whomever you wish but only one of us will speak to you. We can't all speak at the same time. You will feel our presence, and you will be able to discern who is the one who is caressing your face. The Holy Spirit is your companion that walks with you every single second of your life. Whatever Jesus or the Father say, it goes through the Holy Spirit first, and then the Spirit will tell you. Out of the three, not one of us is more than the other. We are all one; we are the same, but yet we are still different. It doesn't matter which one of the three you pray to, just pray. It doesn't matter who you ask, just ask. It doesn't matter who you talk to, just talk. We are not jealous or selfish; we don't fight amongst each other to see who gets the most souls. We are joyful when one of you comes to any of us to pray. We have different functions in your life. The Father says what needs to be done, the Son carries out the Father's request, and the Holy Spirit is the power behind that request. When the sea parted, the Father ordered it to open and Jesus carried out the order and the Spirit was the power that made the ocean part. You can't afford to ignore one; you need all three of us so that we can all work in you."

The Spirit

"I am the vine; you are the branches. If a man remains in me and I in him, he will bear much fruit; apart from me you can do nothing. If anyone does not remain in me, he is like a branch that is thrown away and withers; such branches are picked up, thrown into the fire and burned."

John 15:5–6 (NIV)

10/16/07

"The more one comes to God, the more he or she will realize how perfect God made them. The more you pray, the more you will realize just how Jesus' blood cleansed you. You will come to realize how pure you really are and how God's grace and mercy flows anew every day in your life. You will be in perfect harmony with your Creator, and his flawless love will surround you, but don't let your flesh deceive you. You are only perfect through God, because the Spirit is pure and unstained. But don't let your cleanliness deceive you, because your soul and your flesh are stained by the world. Flesh can never be perfect; it is always stained and sinful. It can't help itself, and it is sinful by nature. The soul fights with the flesh so that it can be cleansed of all filth, but it still remains in the middle of the flesh and the Spirit. The flesh listens to what the soul wants, so then the soul becomes stained when it agrees with the flesh, but the soul has the option to listen to the Spirit. The Spirit will guide the soul into purity, but the soul will eventually find itself in sin, since it is exposed to earthly temptations and desires. So then how can the flesh and the soul ever be perfect? They can't, at least not by themselves. The world will always be influenced by sin. So how can the soul be saved? By the Spirit, which guides you in truth and love, which is Jesus. Without the Spirit the flesh will only exist through the five senses, without the Spirit the soul will only be full of our earthly desires and fears. Your body is only a vessel for your soul and your soul is the connection to the Spirit. In order to conquer the outside world, the inside must be changed to be willing to do as the Spirit sees fit. The Spirit, which is pure, must feed your soul, and only then will your soul benefit and the light will shine from the inside out. You must come to the Father every day, surrender your will to him, let your flesh and your soul go, so that the Spirit can guide you. You can't say 'I will let the Spirit guide me' but then listen to what the flesh has to say. You cannot have two masters. If you are going to let the Spirit guide you, then let it guide you. If you are going to let your soul dominate you, then be careful, because you will have to face the consequences of following your earthly desires. You will expose your weaknesses to the world, and you will be disheartened. Let the Spirit guide you into the perfect will of God. No one will eat an apple that looks delicious on the outside but rotten from within. A seed grows from the inside out, not from the outside in. The ways of the Lord are simple, a seed grows from within us, and it produces good fruit so that the soul and the flesh can nourish themselves. They feed off the seed and grow extensively. You can cut the branches off any tree, but as long as you keep on watering it, the branches will grow back. The leaves can dry and whither away, the wind can try to break the trunk, and the freezing rain will try to stop it from growing, but the fresh water will always come and it will grow once again. If the Spirit is thirsty, then give it drink, and you will see that your soul and your flesh will thank you."

I Have Always Been There

He sought God during the days of Zechariah, who instructed him in the fear of God. As long as he sought the LORD, God gave him success.

2 Chronicles 26:5 (NIV)

10/17/07

"Wash yourself with my blood everyday, bathe in my love that purifies, protect yourself from all evil and temptation, put up your shield to guard you from all the arrows that come hurling at you, and repent from all the sins that you have committed. I did not die in vain, and I did not die so that you could continue to live in defeat. I died to cure to sick, to save the sinner, and so that you could have access to the Father and yet most of you still don't understand the freedom that was given to you that day. I made you worthy when you were unworthy. I made you righteous when you were unrighteous. I made you pure when you were filthy. I made you rich when you were poor. No one can stop you from praying, but yet you still don't pray. No one can stop you from reading the Word, but yet you still don't read. What is happening? Did I not give you freedom so that you could freely befriend me? I have given you authority to conquer the world, but yet you stand still. I have given you the gift of salvation but yet you don't take it. Don't you understand that I am the only way, without me you are lost! So why don't you just ask me to show you the way? Is there an inconvenience in asking you to come and share a meal with me? You have made time for other things; television, going out to eat, work, and school, but you still somehow have managed to put your time for me last. You come to me when it is most convenient or on the other end when times aren't treating you well. Why am I below everything else? You talk about me, you argue about the end of the world, and you try to convert people to come to me, when in fact, you don't follow what you preach. If you want to conquer the world, then you must arm yourselves that you can't expect to win without any weapons. You want the glory but not the struggle, but glory is only achieved after the struggle. You don't have, because you don't ask me. Where are you? I am always waiting, but you don't come. When you finally come, you say that you have found Christ. I never went anywhere. How could you find something that was never lost? What you found was the truth and the way."

Pride

But after Uzziah became powerful, his pride led to his downfall. He was unfaithful to the LORD his God, and entered the temple of the LORD to burn incense on the altar of incense.

2 Chronicles 26:16 (NIV)

10/18/07

"It is of no benefit to your soul to be prideful. Pride is a stone that is in the way of your path towards the Father. Pride doesn't let itself receive love and doesn't know how to forgive. It doesn't truly give and forgets how to ask. Pride has to change, it has to be humbled. The transition hurts, especially when one doesn't realize that it is pride that stands in the way. Pride blinds and deceives; my children cannot let pride run their lives. It's important to let me work in you, because pride will not be contained by your own efforts. Learn to surrender it to me, and I will use it for your benefit. If you try to change by yourself, then you are only fooling yourself. Pride is in the blood, but you cannot feel it. Pride is silent before it attacks, and it will rob you of all spiritual goodness. Ask for change, and I will change you. Ask but don't complain. I need a humble worker to do my will."

The Base

Bear with each other and forgive whatever grievances you may have against one another. Forgive as the Lord forgave you. And over all these virtues put on love, which binds them all together in perfect unity.

Colossians 3:13–14 (NIV)

10/19/07

"Justice is of God, not yours to decide. When someone does you wrong, don't repay with wrong, repay with love. When someone curses you, bless them. But why does God let others treat you ill? Could there be a benefit when someone tries to harm you? Everything around you, whether it seems good or bad, God always uses it for your benefit. Some produce patience while others produce love, wisdom is learned through living. Patience only grows when it is needed. True love only shines when someone doesn't deserve it. A Christian doesn't repay evil with evil, and neither does he cash in on favors. A true follower must be like an assertive servant, knowing when to say 'no' but also always wanting to say 'yes.' If you put yourself up on a cloud, then it will only hurt more when you fall. Let God put you where he sees fit. You must be humble and simple in everything you do. You don't need the praise from others; your only job is to please the Father. The Father's children are the base of the mountain, not the top. People can come and rest on you, and you will help them up. They don't need to climb a mountain to find you. The base is the most important, without it, everything would crumble. The one who thinks he is more is actually less, and the one who thinks he is the lesser will be shown how he can be the greatest."

Pray

Those who led the way rebuked him and told him to be quiet, but he shouted all the more, "Son of David, have mercy on me!" Jesus stopped and ordered the man to be brought to him. When he came near, Jesus asked him, "What do you want me to do for you?" "LORD, I want to see," he replied. Jesus said to him, "Receive your sight; your faith has healed you."

Luke 18:39–42 (NIV)

10/20/07

"The flesh is always going to do what it wants, the flesh deceives you into thinking that it must feel something to realize that the Father is present during your day. Train your flesh to listen to your soul and in turn listen to the Spirit so that you could feed the soul. Like I said before, I don't reside in your feelings, and don't depend on your five senses in order to know that I am there. Rather, depend on the Spirit that encompasses all understanding, and you will realize that feelings have no part in the spiritual realm. Just because you can't feel anything, it doesn't mean that nothing is happening. On the contrary, everything is rearranging around you and in you. This is because when you pray in Spirit, the soul and flesh become secondary. That is why your flesh doesn't feel anything when you pray. Don't let your flesh deceive you when you pray. Sometimes I let you feel my presence and other times you don't need to, but it doesn't mean I'm not there or that I don't listen. When you pray, you need faith—since you are asking for something that you might not see yet or you don't know how it can come to pass. If you could see me and feel me all the time, then of what use would faith be? In order to have faith, you must pray and listen to my Word, but you must also learn to pray in faith. Prayer and faith are intertwined; you can't have one without the other."

Necessity

"Everything is permissible"—but not everything is beneficial.
"Everything is permissible"—but not everything is constructive.
Nobody should seek his own good, but the good of others.

1 Corinthians 10:23–24 (NIV)

10/21/07

"It is not practical to feel depressed when your God is with you, it is not practical to grow impatient when your God takes care of you, and it is not practical to fear when your God protects you. Many things aren't necessary in your lives, but yet you have learned to make them a part of our routine. The only thing necessary in your life is to be with your Lord. The only thing that should be running through your mind is 'What does God need me to do?' You are children of the King, and as children, there are certain duties that must be accomplished. Don't busy yourselves with things that bring you no benefit; busy yourselves with things that will enhance my kingdom. Take advantage of today, spend time with those you love, but remember to come to me when you wake so that my wisdom and peace will flow through you. Before you sleep come and rest your troubles on my pillow of comfort. Appreciate that I am with you. You must learn to die so that I can live in you."

Brag

For by him all things were created: things in heaven and on earth, visible and invisible, whether thrones or powers or rulers or authorities; all things were created by him and for him. He is before all things, and in him all things hold together.

Colossians 1:16–17 (NIV)

10/22/07

"All the material possessions you have are only because the Father has allowed you to have them. All the spiritual gifts that you utilize are only because the Father has permitted you to have them. All the power that has been entrusted to you is only because the Father has lent it to you. Then if everything comes through the Father, if everything is given through him and nothing out of your own works can bring you anything, then you have nothing to brag about that has not been given. You can work all day and all night, but in the end, if the Father doesn't allow you to have it, then you never will. In all your work, realize that everything is given because of his grace. Your works can only take you as far as your faith but they cannot save you, and if you believe that the Father has better plans for you, then your strength and your works will no longer be focused to satisfy yourself, they will come together for your Father who is in heaven. Well then how can those who don't believe in God or in Christ be so successful? The Father permits it, but they are fooled into thinking that it was only through their works that they have come to be successful; they ignore the grace that God has given them. God gives us everything—food, clothes, money, strength, and faith—but we have to put our part. Everything is allowed, and the amount is unlimited, but not everything is approved and yet some have more and some have less. Don't let the world measure you by your earthly possessions, for those who have more but don't have the Lord, in reality, have nothing. Those who have less but have the Lord, have more than all the riches combined. Success is not measured by money, fortune, fame; true success is doing God's will to the best of your ability and with a grateful heart. It's not good to brag about your possessions, since they aren't really yours. You're just borrowing them for a while. If you're going to brag about something, brag about my kingdom and brag about my love. If you ask me, I will give it to you. You were made to be stewards of the King therefore having access to the King's palace and riches."

When You Die

Set your minds on things above, not on earthly things. For you died, and your life is now hidden with Christ in God. When Christ, who is your life, appears, then you also will appear with him in glory.

Colossians 3:2–4 (NIV)

"When your self dies you realize that your prayers change, you realize that what once seemed important to you now seem insignificant. When your self dies then that is when you really begin to live. When you open your eyes to the Spirit, he will guide you into his will, and your actions will reflect on it. When you surrender to me your ego, your prayers become the will of the Father, because God can't work in you when you are always listening to your flesh. The flesh is weak, but the Spirit is strong. The flesh is always looking to satisfy its earthly appetite, but the Spirit does what needs to be done. When your self dies the world will change color and the Word will no longer just be the word but it will be the life and that life will live in you. You will be consumed by the Word, and you will consume the Word, and forever be united in love. Your life is the Word being represented here on earth; you are no longer guided by your flesh but by the Word. You are both one, joined by faith and sealed in love. Where one is, surely the other is as well."

Wisdom

Once, having been asked by the Pharisees when the kingdom of God would come, Jesus replied, "The kingdom of God does not come with your careful observation, nor will people say, 'Here it is,' or 'There it is,' because the kingdom of God is within you."

Luke 17:20–21 (NIV)

10/23/07

"One day, your eyes will be opened, and you will see that earthly wisdom is but superficial. One day many things will be revealed to you, and you will be amazed at how many things have been in front of you but yet you missed to see them. The things of God are simple but can be made difficult, they are in plain sight, but hidden. They speak, but are not heard. If you ask, I will show you. If you ask, I will teach you. There are many wonders to be discovered but very little time. The secrets that have been shown to you, it is good that you share them so that others can believe and be joyful in the treasures that are given. There is a thirst that I put in you so that you can keep on searching but that thirst only comes after you have been willing to come and drink from the water of life. When you are walking through the desert, I give you drink, and the more you walk the more drink I give you. You walk in search of wisdom, and I like that, because anything that you pursue with a diligent heart I will give you. Everything is hidden, simply because you can't run before you crawl. Learn to crawl, and I will show you how to run. Learn to walk with me, and then I will share with you my secrets so that you can learn and understand. All things revealed are permitted because I love you, but you have to let me guide you so that you can see the world through my eyes. The wise are fools, because they satisfy only themselves, they forget the giver of wisdom. They don't study to know me, they study just to get to know about me. In all their knowledge, they know nothing if they don't know me, of what purpose is wisdom if it is not utilized correctly? True wisdom can only come through serving your Creator. Any child of mine that wants to know the Father will be shown the light where there is darkness. A child learns out of love and respect, I am willing to give only if you are willing to receive. The more you know me, the more you will know yourself. The more you seek me, the more you will seek yourself. Only through heavenly wisdom can you apply heavenly knowledge."

Come Home

"'My son,' the father said, 'you are always with me, and everything I have is yours. But we had to celebrate and be glad, because this brother of yours was dead and is alive again; he was lost and is found.'"

Luke 15:31–32 (NIV)

10/24/07

"The more obedient you are, the more susceptive you will be to hearing my voice. The sheep know the shepherd's voice. The farther away the sheep stray from the flock, the more difficult it becomes to hear the master's voice. The good thing is that no matter how far the sheep wander, they can always come back and be accepted as if they never left. Like the prodigal son, a great feast is held for all those who come back to their Father. I am your house, and you should know that my door is always open to those willing to come. Don't be afraid or ashamed; I will always be at the door waiting for you. You won't even have a chance to knock at my door before I come to you. I will take care of your needs, I will dress you, I will give you drink, I will feed you, and I will guide you and give you what you need. It doesn't matter where you went or where you were going, the important thing is where will you go after you have stayed at my house. I know that the world can mistreat you, especially if you are alone and lost, but I'll tell you something. Even though you felt alone, I was always there trying to guide you into my love. Come home, my son. Come and have a seat with your Father."

Thirst

"But when he, the Spirit of truth, comes, he will guide you into all truth. He will not speak on his own; he will speak only what he hears, and he will tell you what is yet to come."

John 16:13 (NIV)

10/25/07

"You thirst and hunger for things that only I can give you. That thirst is not of the flesh but of the Spirit. The impatience towards knowledge of my kingdom is good, the search to understand and to learn about me will take your whole life and still you will lack many things. Remember that my Spirit is here to guide you and help you because there are so many things that can bring no benefit but the Spirit knows all things. Let the Holy Spirit guide you, there will be no end to the wisdom that I give you; there will be no end to the treasures that you will find. He is a force that will make my power shine through you. He is the author of great ideas. He is the miracle worker in all of you. Pray before you read and my light will shine where there was darkness before."

Patience

Be still before the LORD and wait patiently for him; do not fret when men succeed in their ways, when they carry out their wicked schemes.

Psalm 37:7 (NIV)

10/26/07

"The world is always in a hurry, it's always saying, 'What time is it? I'm late, and I need to go.' They want everything fast, everything when they ask. The world has made you a slave to impatience. You want answers immediately; you want to know the 'why' behind everything. Impatience starts to become part of your life, and when you least expect it, you begin to lose sleep. You can't find rest. You always have to go somewhere only to comeback to go somewhere else. You haven't finished with something when you want to do something else. We must work together to get rid of this impatience in your lives; it brings you no benefit whatsoever. It only brings frustration and doubt. How can you trust me if you don't wait for me? I don't work around your time, I don't work only when you ask. I work when I want. It's that simple. If I don't want to do something, then I won't do it, but you have to understand that everything is for your benefit and on my time. Just because nothing seems to be happening when you asked, it doesn't mean that I am not doing something to help you. Just because you think that I didn't hear your petition doesn't mean that I ignored you. I listen to my children when they speak, I am always willing to give and make you happy but you must understand that sometimes I have better plans for you. Plans that exceed your expectations are always being wrapped waiting for you to open them. Don't lose hope, don't fear, and don't be impatient for the promises that I gave you. I always keep my word, but you have to trust me. I never go back on my word, and I never regret what I say. Just keep on believing and speaking the words of truth, you will see how everything that you didn't know you wished will come to pass."

Feelings

Therefore we are always confident and know that as long as we are at home in the body we are away from the LORD. We live by faith, not by sight.

2 Corinthians 5:6–7 (NIV)

"When the Spirit is shining in you, you will find out that the desires of the flesh are not as attractive as they once seemed. Your feelings seem to be a bit more distant when it comes to worldly desires, because you are beginning to live in the Spirit. You are not guided by your flesh anymore, and the more you let the Spirit guide you, the less you will be carried away by your emotions. This doesn't mean that you won't feel a thing, but what it does mean is that you will be able to make decisions based on truth and knowledge, not by blind opinions. Your emotions should not control your decisions, you must let your ego go and let the Spirit flow. Your spiritual eyes will see things that were once hidden to your physical eyes. Your mouth will be unable to speak ill because the Spirit will be guiding you in what to say. You will be observing yourself through the inside out, and your ears will finally be able to hear me more clearly and you will feel me when I breathe. We are intimate friends, and as such, we must spend time together and share each other's secrets. In the spiritual world, your senses are useless, you don't need them to know that I am near you."

Break

For you, O Lord, have delivered my soul from death, my eyes from tears, my feet from stumbling, that I may walk before the Lord in the land of the living.

Psalm 116:8–9 (NIV)

10/27/07

"We must break the chains that imprison you, we must purify your soul, we must change the impure into pure, and you must get rid of all your sin and fear that pushes you away from me. How? By accepting what Christ did for you. Through obedience and by doing my will you can walk without stumbling. Even if you don't understand the how, you must understand that the ability to change your life is your choice. You can only become pure if you obey and surrender completely to me. I don't force anyone to receive me, but the impurities must be washed away from your soul. It might hurt, but there is no shortcut around it. True knowledge is sometimes painful. I test you and try you, and each of you is different. I never treat any two alike. Don't just listen to those things that you prefer, but listen to those things that will help you grow. I don't work in your life out of your convenience; I work in what is necessary at the time. Learn to leave everything in my time, leave everything in my hands and rest. You may need to pass through fire but only to not be burned later. You need to wash yourselves with my grace, even when you think you don't need it. Only the Creator can see the hidden flaws in his masterpiece. Only the Creator can see what is holding you back. A child of mine doesn't follow me out of convenience but rather out of love, and out of that love flows convenience for your life. You are children of the highest King; you are children of the Most High. Let go of your doubts. I don't want to be telling you over and over again. Learn to be obedient with the small things, and I will grant you more and more."

Leader

"For everyone who exalts himself will be humbled, and he who humbles himself will be exalted."

Luke 14:11 (NIV)

10/28/07

"A leader is not one who seeks attention by seating in the important places. A true leader is the one who sits among everyone and enjoys the company of others. A leader is not the one who gives the most money but rather one that shares what he has, whether it be little or much. A leader doesn't seek the approval of everyone but rather the approval of the Father, the blessing of the Son, and the guidance of the Spirit. Respect is not gained by your position; it is earned by your character. Love is not given out of fear but rather by choice. A leader can't believe he is the most important; he must be humble and filled with compassion. Jesus could have been born an earthly king, he could have sat with the highest officials, and he could have chosen to be with 'high' society. But what did he do? He chose to be born in a humble house and become the son of a carpenter. He taught that the base is more important than the peak, he showed humbleness, that money isn't everything, but most important of all, he showed that it doesn't matter where you come from as long as you know where you are going. God has a plan for everyone. The amount of money that you have is of no importance; God supplies everyone's needs. It doesn't matter if you're not a great speaker, because God will put words in your mouth. The color of your skin doesn't matter. The only color that Christ cares to see is the color of love. Don't let your past hinder you but rather learn from it. A true leader knows that it is only through the Father that he got to where he is today."

Pain

But now that you have been set free from sin and have become slaves to God, the benefit you reap leads to holiness, and the result is eternal life. For the wages of sin is death, but the gift of God is eternal life in Christ Jesus our LORD.

Romans 6:22–23 (NIV)

10/29/07

"Is pain necessary in your life? Yes, but there are different types of pain. The first one is the one that you cause between yourselves. This one is based on your poor decisions when you decide that you know the way and you ignore my counsel. You base your decisions on worldly desires, and in the end, it only brings you more heartache than joy. Frustration sets in, and you begin to feel lost, you begin to feel alone and no one seems to bring you comfort. Worry doesn't let you sleep, and you find yourself desperate for a change. There is also physical pain when you let anger turn into rage and end up hurting someone or sometimes yourself. There are so many hurts that are not necessary in your life, but you create them. You let them reign in your life as if they belong there in the first place. I let everything happen, but understand that you make choices that sometimes are based on selfishness. Those choices only bring regret. The other type of pain is the one that is necessary in order to grow in love. In the beginning, it may seem very painful, but it is the most beneficial. When a child of mine comes and asks for a complete makeover in their life, you must get ready, because I must chip away everything that brings you unnecessary pain. The soul must be cleansed, but it can only be cleansed when it is passed through the fire. The selfishness will burn, as well as many other things that stand in your way of growing. Your whole self must be thoroughly washed and cleansed, but it must begin with the inside, let the fountain of life flow to the outskirts. This is the only way to truly be cleansed and come to be one with the Father, having your soul washed by the Holy Spirit after accepting Jesus as your King. Changes are always inconvenient, but understand that I am molding and reshaping the metal that structures your way of life. I know that you sometimes resist, but what this does is make the process extend beyond the normal time frame. When you ask for change, it doesn't happen overnight, but I use the situations in your life to make you realize your weaknesses. After you realize what your weakness is, then you can let me work on it. Do not fear for it is required to live a free and healthy life. You will see that I am always in control. Don't fear change, fear not changing."

Baptized by the Spirit

So I say, live by the Spirit, and you will not gratify the desires of the sinful nature. For the sinful nature desires what is contrary to the Spirit, and the Spirit what is contrary to the sinful nature. They are in conflict with each other, so that you do not do what you want.

Galatians 5:16–17 (NIV)

10/30/07

"In your conscience lies reasoning, everyone is born with the capacity to understand good from evil. The Holy Spirit is in everyone, the difference is that some invite him in, and others leave him knocking at the door. The Holy Spirit won't push his will on you; he won't force himself on your life. You have to invite him to have divine guidance. If you want to learn how to read the Word, if you want to have a more efficient prayer, or if you want to heal the sick through God's power, then you need the Holy Spirit to live in you. You need to let him guide you in everything from a simple decision to the difficulties you might face. When you receive Jesus as your personal savior, it is only the first step. Yes, Jesus is the only way to reach the Father, and Jesus will transform your life. Salvation comes through him and sanctification comes through the Spirit. You have to surrender to the will of the Spirit, leave the flesh for the flesh and live in the spirit for the Spirit. When Jesus went up, he left you a friend to console and to teach you. Without the Spirit there can be no spiritual change in your life. The same way you invite Christ, you have to invite the Holy Spirit. The way you are baptized by water, you also have to be baptized by the Spirit. You have to eat the fruit of the Spirit every day and drink from the water of life that is freely given. Without Christ, you can't be saved, and without the Spirit, you can't produce good fruit."

Judge

Let us not become weary in doing good, for at the proper time
we will reap a harvest if we do not give up.

Galatians 6:9 (NIV)

10/31/07

"The world is quick to judge and slow to forgive. It is always the
fault of the other for which you remember them by. It is rare that
you remember the greatness of someone without mentioning their
weakness. Why? Why does the world like to focus on the imperfec-
tions? The world likes to believe that perfection is not possible, even
when someone comes around and performs great deeds. The world
looks for the hidden fault instead of revealing the triumph. And
when they finally find it, the world breathes easier and they console
themselves saying, 'Of course, she is a great servant of God. But did
you know that she was in jail?' Always judging, always looking for
the fall of their fellow brother or sister. The more you set your eyes
on the flaw of others, the less you will be able to see what path you
are traveling on. All my children are imperfect but are made perfect.
Everyone has blemishes in their lives, but my grace wraps them with
love and perfection. The world only sees through worldly eyes, but
I see you with the eyes of the Spirit and love. I see your heart, pure
and noble. I examine your mind, full of wisdom and knowledge.
I see your love simple and incorruptible. Don't let the flesh judge
your spirit. It is difficult to please everyone, especially when they

don't understand that my children also have feelings of their own. I know you sometimes get upset, I know that you cry, and I know that you sometimes feel disappointed, but in the end, no one said that there weren't rocks on the road. Don't the blind judge you by what they see, don't let the mute speak ill of you, and don't let the deaf only hear what they want to hear. Just be thankful at all times to the Father who brings life. Give yourself to God, and he will give himself to you. The things of the Father are eternal and the things of the world are only brief."

These are the words of God.

Conclusion

Let us remember that we shouldn't forget to fear the Lord as well as to love him. To thank him for everything we have and be grateful for the things we will have. God gives us according to his good purpose, and it is only until later that we are able to see why it seemed that God didn't answer our prayer. In God, there is no darkness; he is the eternal light that shines where there seemed to be no hope. We comprehend that he is our King, and as our King, he deserves our outmost respect and honor.

This book has made its way into your life for one simple reason: to transform you. Everything that you were is no more, everything that you wished to be can still be attained, except this time, you won't travel alone. His words are written on paper but seeped in into our soul. His love holding our insecurity and giving us hope. His forgiveness erases our guilt and forgets our sins. We behave as if we don't need God and we have become absorbed into our own lives that we have lost sight of the true meaning of life. We have walked away from God but yet he still waits. He loved us first and we forgot him second. God is yearning for his children to come back to their Father. Let his love be poured out into your life. He is the divine, he is the Word, he is the revelation. Without God we don't deserve anything but with him we inherit everything. It is never too late to love and to be loved.

Receive Jesus Christ

> "When a man believes in me, he does not believe in me only, but in the one who sent me. When he looks at me, he sees the one who sent me. I have come into the world as a light, so that no one who believes in me should stay in darkness."
>
> John 12:44–46, (NIV)

It doesn't matter where you come from or what you did, what matters is where you decide to go from here. God sent his Son so that everyone can have eternal life but that's not all. Only through Jesus can we receive supernatural healing in our soul, in our body, in our finances, but better yet we can start a loving relationship with God that will blossom and spread to your friends, your family, your co-workers, your enemies and everything around you. Only through the grace of salvation can we truly be set free from our sinful nature. Jesus paid the price so that we wouldn't have to. All you have to do is pray this simple prayer and believe it and you will receive Jesus as your personal savior.

"Jesus I confess that you are my King and my Savior, I repent of all the sins that I've done, it doesn't matter what I did or wanted to do but now I summit myself to your will in my life. Cleanse me with your precious love and renew my mind, my heart, and my soul. I believe that you are alive in me and I in you. I receive your salvation and what you did for me at the cross. Amen."

Receive the Holy Spirit

> May the grace of the Lord Jesus Christ, and the love of God, and the fellowship of the Holy Spirit be with you all.
>
> 2 Corinthians 13:14, (NIV)

What a great honor it is to be called sons of God but it is yet a greater honor that God wants to be part of our everyday lives. The Holy Spirit wants to be involved in every affair of our schedules but he also wants for him to be our schedule. He is waiting to share with you the secrets of God but like his Son we must welcome him into our lives. The Holy Spirit will lead us into unknown paths that have a tremendous amount of wisdom, revelation, and power. He will never force his will upon us but we must yield to his advice and counsel. When we receive Jesus into our hearts we must also invite the Holy Spirit to be a part of our lives.

"I surrender my will and my weaknesses to you Holy Spirit, I accept you and invite you into my life. I accept the responsibility of sharing the fruit of your wisdom and power. I thank you for transforming my life and those around me. Help me share the truth of the Word, the truth of the Son and the Father. I open myself to your guidance. Let your power flow through me. In Jesus name, Amen."

Our Mission

We are God's army. We are his representatives here on earth. We must light the way amidst the darkness for those who have strayed from the truth. God has given us the responsibility to spread his Word. If one is willing, God will provide. If one is believing, God will show up. We must get up and march. We must stand proud and lift our heads high in humbleness for we are sons of God. Jesus redeemed us so that we can stand and fight. Our strength comes from above from an everlasting supply. It's time to take up our sword, dust the dirt off our hair and take our place. We must help the needy, feed the poor, and let God show his love through us. We can save the world one soul at a time.

Follow us on Facebook:

Ruben Gabriel - A Divine Word From A Revelation
Or contact us: thesentinelsofGod@gmail.com

listen|imagine|view|experience

AUDIO BOOK DOWNLOAD INCLUDED WITH THIS BOOK!

In your hands you hold a complete digital entertainment package. In addition to the paper version, you receive a free download of the audio version of this book. Simply use the code listed below when visiting our website. Once downloaded to your computer, you can listen to the book through your computer s speakers, burn it to an audio CD or save the file to your portable music device (such as Apple s popular iPod) and listen on the go!

How to get your free audio book digital download:

1. Visit www.tatepublishing.com and click on the e|LIVE logo on the home page.
2. Enter the following coupon code:
   b314-bad3-fddf-c551-fb9b-8e65-c3b7-dcf8
3. Download the audio book from your e|LIVE digital locker and begin enjoying your new digital entertainment package today!